N C O I L A S

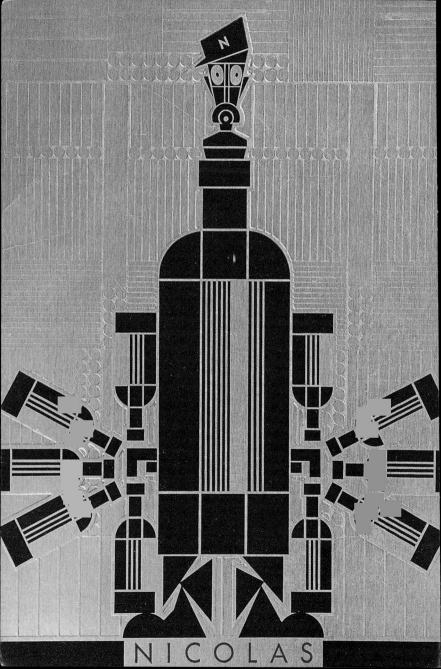

NICOLAS

CONTENTS

GRAPHICS
A CENTURY OF POSTER AND ADVERTISING DESIGN

Alain Weill

Thames & Hudson

'Commercial graphic design: the term did not exist fifteen years ago, although the activity it describes is ancient. The emergence of a group of graphic artists specializing in this domain is associated with the global expansion of the world of business and commerce, accompanied by a tremendous growth in industrial power, as well as by determining factors in the fields of politics and culture, which are now more closely linked with current events than ever.'

Fritz H. Ehmcke, 'Deutsche Gebrauchsgraphik', in *Klimschs Jahrbuch Frankfurt*, 1927

CHAPTER 1

THE BIRTH OF GRAPHIC DESIGN

In 1898, Henry van de Velde began to create a series of decorative framing devices for the food company Tropon, consisting of whiplash patterns of interlocking lines. These were adapted for use on the firm's posters and packaging (opposite). Soon afterwards, in Berlin, Lucian Bernhard created a range of simple graphic designs for Manoli cigarettes (earlier packaging shown left: Bernhard's designs above).

The origins of graphic design lie in the revolution in the decorative arts. Until the early 19th century, levels of production went more or less hand in hand with limited levels of demand. Within the space of a few decades, however, progress in many fields – the power of coal, steam-driven machinery, advances in physics and chemistry, electricity and a host of new inventions marketed by dynamic entrepreneurs – brought about a radical and fundamental transformation of Western economies. Abetted by a rapidly growing rail network, the cities and their industrial suburbs swallowed up large sections of the rural population. At the same time, the imperialist powers of Europe were acquiring wealth from their colonies on an unprecedented scale.

Advances in printing

Developments in printing processes accelerated at an equally breakneck speed. The lithographic process, invented by Senefelder in 1796 and perfected by Engelmann, improved from year to year, making it easier to produce large-scale images. The raw material – paper made from wood pulp refined using a technique developed by Henry Voelter in 1846, plus products including chlorine – was available in huge rolls at low cost. In this form, it could be used on the automatic presses invented by Friedrich Koenig, who, with Andreas Bauer, introduced improvements culminating in machines that were capable of printing over a thousand sheets per hour. Aluminium and zinc replacements for the stone bed used in the lithographic process increased the speed of printing still further, as did the development of the rotating cylinder press.

In the early 1860s, Firmin Gillot began to experiment with photo-relief printing, and in 1886 Ottmar Mergenthaler, working in America, developed the keyboard-operated Linotype machine, revolutionizing the printing of newspapers and books. The Monotype

Setting type by hand was a long, laborious and costly process. The first patent for a type composing machine was registered in 1825, but it was not until 1886 that

Otto Mergenthaler, a German immigrant in New York (above, seated), developed the first machine that really worked. Activated by a keyboard, brass matrices of the letterforms slid into order; these were then filled with molten lead, which solidified to form raised type. This new 'Linotype' process meant that one operator could now do the work of several compositors. The process reduced the production costs of newspapers and books and so increased their circulation.

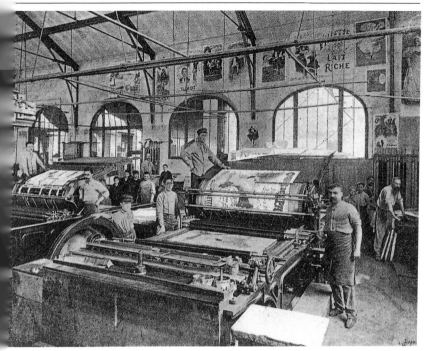

machine, first patented by an American, Tolbert Lanston, in 1896, remained in use until the 1970s. In 1905, Ira Rubel invented the offset printing process, in which a rubber roller economized on inking.

The 'total work of art'

While scientific and technical advances offered ever-increasing potential at ever-diminishing costs, industrial manufacturers were content to mass-produce mediocre, conventional items, remaining impervious to creativity in any form. It was this relentless domination of the market by formulaic pastiches of existing styles that caused a reaction throughout the industrialized West.

The Arts and Crafts movement in England, founded by William Morris in 1861, Art Nouveau in France and Belgium, and its German manifestation Jugendstil, were all united in their rejection of the imitation of tired styles in favour of a return to the creative approach of

In the second half of the 19th century, advances in lithographic printing boosted the rise of the poster. Huge presses (above) made it possible to print formats as large as 120 x 160 cm (47 x 63 in.), using flat stones weighing several hundred kilos. Manoeuvring these great stones was a delicate business, however, and they were soon replaced by a metal sheet mounted on a rotary press. This reduced not only the size of the presses but also the number of workers needed to operate them.

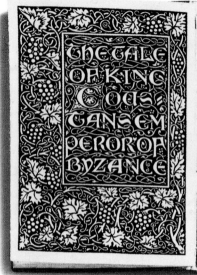

medieval craftsmen. It is no coincidence that the chief theorists of this movement – Morris himself, Henry van de Velde, Peter Behrens, Joseph Maria Olbrich, Josef Hoffmann and Charles Rennie Mackintosh – were all architects, working in the discipline that, more than any other, united all the branches of the decorative arts. This concept of the *Gesamtkunstwerk* or 'total work of art', all-encompassing as it was in its application, led these artists quite naturally to embrace typography and advertising art in all its forms on equal terms.

Britain: cradle of innovation

The first country in Europe to experience an industrial revolution, Britain was also the first (in 1837) to open a school of design, and (in 1853) a museum devoted specifically to the decorative arts: the South Kensington Museum, later to become the Victoria & Albert Museum. By the same token, it was also the first to be faced with the problems of adjustment posed by the revolution in manufacturing industry, as was revealed inescapably by the Great Exhibition of 1851. While the glass-and-steel construction of the Crystal Palace itself

Guiding light of the Arts and Crafts Movement and practitioner of all the decorative arts, William Morris (above) devoted his energies to making books from 1891, founding the Kelmscott Press which became influential throughout the world.

was clearly revolutionary, the multitude of exhibits it housed were quite a different matter, a dispiriting hotchpotch of pastiches of every possible historical style. For Marx and Engels, the exhibition was 'striking proof of the concentrated power with which modern large-scale industry is everywhere demolishing national barriers and increasingly blurring local peculiarities of production, society and national character among all peoples'. The critic and social commentator John Ruskin, who likened the Crystal Palace itself to a giant cucumber frame, also condemned the materialism of the Victorian age, championing in its place a sorely needed revival of craftsmanship in the arts.

It was William Morris and the Arts and Crafts movement who were to put Ruskin's theories into practice. Seeking a return to pure creative expression, with the Middle Ages as his model, Morris rejected the distinction between artist and craftsman. From here it was but a step to the wholesale rejection of mechanization, mass production and industrialization in all its forms. A passionate devotee of all the decorative arts and especially textiles, Morris founded the Kelmscott Press in 1891: using a traditional hand press, he set about producing masterpieces of printing and book design, for which he also designed his own typefaces: Golden, Troy and Chaucer. Other like-minded artists followed suit, notably Arthur Mackmurdo, who set up the Century Guild, and Walter Crane, later to become the first president of the Arts and Crafts Society. Morris's ideas became a catalyst for all decorative arts movements throughout the world, and his use of decorative motifs inspired by plant forms became hugely influential in the

The title page from *The Tale of King Constans Emperor of Byzance* (1896; opposite above) shows the detail and sophistication of Morris's approach, and the degree to which he was influenced by medieval Books of Hours. His disciple Arthur Mackmurdo, himself influenced by the Italian Renaissance and a passion for plant forms and Japanese art, founded the Century Guild in 1882. The exuberant organic forms of his title page for *Wren's City Churches* (1883; below) look forward to Art Nouveau. Mackmurdo influenced artists such as Henry van de Velde and Otto Eckmann, who designed a stylized title page for John Ruskin's *Seven Lamps of Architecture* (*c.* 1900; left).

development of Art Nouveau. But his implacable hostility to mechanization was in the end his downfall, ensuring that in practice his works became elitist and were accessible only to a privileged few. As Claude Roger-Marx noted with cruel accuracy, 'They lost themselves in the dark night of the past in order to illumine the future.'

The Victorian era

Outside these small and rarefied circles, Victorian Britain was fundamentally reactionary. Advertising art was remarkable chiefly for its mediocrity, with manufacturers contenting themselves with reproducing paintings by establishment artists such as Sir John Millais, whose *Bubbles* for Pears Soap was the very antithesis of graphic art.

Aubrey Beardsley, whose meteoric career was cut short by his early death at the age of twenty-five, created a scandal in 1894 with his poster for the Avenue Theatre, the first graphic image to display the Japanese influence that later informed his designs for *The Yellow Book* and *The Savoy*. James Pryde and William Nicholson, two young artists who worked together as the Beggarstaff Brothers, continued Toulouse-Lautrec's explorations into Japanese forms and, using the new technique of collage, created designs based on areas of flat colour that are still startlingly powerful and modern in their impact. In Glasgow, meanwhile, a new school of design emerged which broke all links with the past in order to create a new art of a purity that became one of the inspirations behind the Vienna Secession. Charles Rennie Mackintosh and Herbert McNair, two of its leading proponents, were true modernists.

The Arts and Crafts movement had been the first to grapple with the notion of a creative revival: now it was up to the rest of the world to develop it.

Paris: artists to the fore

Although France had adopted industrialization with an alacrity equal to that of Great Britain, it lagged behind when it came to raising the status of the decorative arts.

Although he had many detractors, Aubrey Beardsley (posters above) was hailed by M. H. Spielmann in *The Modern Poster* (1895) as 'a draughtsman of weird and singular power', who 'showed a deep natural instinct for the beauty of line, for the balance of chiaroscuro, and for decorative effect'. He influenced an entire generation, including Will Bradley.

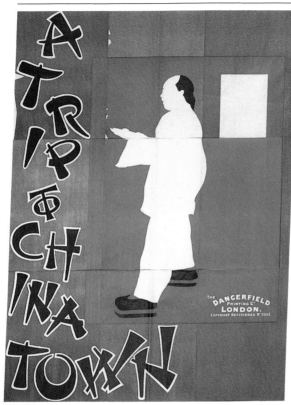

One of the few posters produced by the Beggarstaff Brothers, *A Trip to Chinatown* (opposite), illustrates all the features that made their work revolutionary for its time: the use of a collage of paper cut-outs with no outlines, the white areas left unprinted, and typography of exhilarating freedom. Equally significant, though in a different vein, is the poster by Margaret and Frances Macdonald and Herbert NcNair for the Glasgow Institute of the Fine Arts (below); its spare lines and geometric structure heralded the end of ornamental extravagance.

Not until 1880 was the Union Centrale des Arts Décoratifs established, and the museum that it opened in the Marsan wing of the Louvre in 1905 was anything but modern. Roger-Marx deplored the fact that that it was 'neither free of charge nor lit in the evening, with galleries hardly distinguishable from those of the Louvre'.

Any forward-thinking projects aimed at resolving 'the ancient rivalry between the arts and crafts' – including the Comte de Laborde's famous report of 1851 – came to nothing. The state remained firmly rooted in the era of the great factories such as Sèvres and Gobelins, 'relics of the Ancien Régime, incoherent wrecks of courtly excess'. Disdaining the applied arts, France remained the home

of fine art, and indeed considered itself its sole repository. But while the Academy triumphed at the Salon, on its fringes Impressionism paved the way for a whole generation of artists who, having passed through the studios of painters such as Cormon, Bonnat and Cabanel and found inspiration in the works of Degas, Manet and Gauguin, sought different paths.

From the mid-19th century, the work of Jules Chéret started to raise the status of posters and of advertising art in general. In the romantic period, France had begun to produce posters of considerable artistic quality for booksellers to advertise new publications. The black-and-white lithographs of Paul Gavarni, Denis-Auguste Raffet and Tony Johannot, and in particular Edouard Manet's masterly design illustrating Champfleury's *Les Chats* (1868), clearly indicate that there was a commercial gap to be filled, which Chéret broadened to include the fields of the theatre and business. With his early poster for the opera *Orphée aux enfers* in 1858, he developed the chromolithographic process, using only black and the three primary colours (red, yellow and blue) and so requiring only four lithographic stones.

This represented a genuine revolution: for the first time, large colour images were put on display in public thoroughfares, freely on view to the public. Now posters for aperitifs jostled with advertisements for lamp oil and

The stage curtain at Les Ambassadeurs (above right) shows the prolific nature of Chéret's output in the 1890s. Dubbed the 'Watteau of the streets' and loved by the critics, he produced variations on his *Chérette* girls for the major advertisers of the day (above left).

Toulouse-Lautrec was appointed as Chéret's successor in 1891 by Zidler, director of the Moulin Rouge (opposite below), and introduced a radical new approach. Chéret's allegories (opposite below, inset) yielded to Toulouse-Lautrec's realistic interiors (opposite above). Flourishes of colour gave way to pools of white paper, transformed into La Goulue's petticoats, and the colour black was reintroduced.

fiercely competitive novelties such as bicycles. Chéret also introduced or established two other principles: the regular use of the female form (his pretty girls were dubbed *Chérettes*) in advertising, and – more subtly – the repetition of the same image with variations. His work for Saxoléine lamp oil in particular anticipated the modern concept of the advertising campaign.

Grasset and Mucha, pioneers of Art Nouveau

Paris was in its heyday. City of the arts, centre of luxury goods, pleasure and entertainment, it embraced the art of the poster with careless frivolity, and hundreds of other artists now followed in Chéret's footsteps, each with his own individual style. Eugène Grasset was familiar with the Arts and Crafts movement, and like other artists of his generation had discovered Japanese

A paper sketch is transferred on to each of the stones by the artist: he never squares up first. He indicates the half-tones with a lithographic pencil, and ink allows him to create solidity and trace the drawing's basic outlines. There is one stone for each primary colour: red, yellow and blue. These three plates are sometimes completed by a fourth, to make the greys richer: it is through the opposition or superimposition of the basic tones that every possible variation of shade is obtained. When the artist distributes his reds, he is thinking of how they will change when the yellows are laid on top of them, and how they will both change when the blues are added to dull them or make them more intense.

Achille Segard
on the lithographer
Jules Chéret

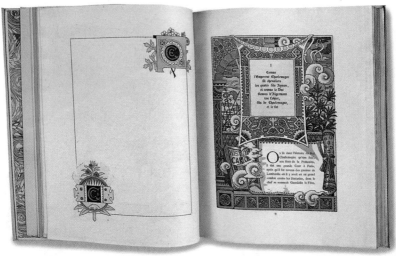

ABCDEFGHIJKLM
ABCDEFGHIJKLM
NOPQRSTUVXYZ
NOPQRSTUVXYZ

Grasset was a major name in French Art Nouveau. Inspired by the Arts and Crafts movement, he revolutionized book design and technology with his design for *Histoire des Quatre Fils*

art, first exhibited in France at the Exposition Universelle of 1867 and popularized by *ukiyo-e* prints. He also found inspiration in the fauna and flora of the French countryside, showing an attention to detail worthy of medieval craftsmen. He designed furniture, stained glass and jewelry, but it was in the field of graphic design that his influence was greatest. His illustrations for *Histoire des Quatre Fils Aymon* (1883) were technologically innovative (they used a colour photo-relief process developed by publisher Charles Gillot) and embodied an entirely new approach to book design. In his posters, meanwhile, Grasset established the stereotype of the Symbolist woman, with serpentine locks and strongly outlined features, as though drawn in stained glass. As well as teaching, he and his followers Verneuil and Berthon published highly influential books of decorative

Aymon (above). Based on medieval Books of Hours, he conceived layout designs for each page which blended text, illustrations and decorative motifs into a harmonious whole. He also designed rather austere typefaces, while his colleague Georges Auriol produced more flowing characters inspired by Japanese brush strokes (see the comparison of Grasset and Auriol faces above). His fonts Provençale and Auriol are still widely used today.

floral motifs, as also espoused by Gallé and
the Nancy School. The typeface he designed,
Grasset, and that designed by his colleague
Auriol, both became hallmarks of this period.

In 1895, Alphonse Mucha's *Gismonda* poster
for Sarah Bernhardt signified the arrival of a
great poster artist, who worked in a style of
byzantine flamboyance that raised French Art
Nouveau to new heights. With their depictions
of extravagantly flowing tresses and their
dazzling ornamentation, Mucha's posters
and graphics were technical and artistic
masterpieces. His virtuoso career as a poster
designer, working not only for theatres but
also for all the major advertising companies,
spanned a mere five years, but his publications
(such as *Documents Décoratifs*), his illustrations
for books (including *Ilsée, Princesse de Tripoli*)
and his jewelry designs and store interior for
Georges Fouquet influenced a generation.

Paris celebrates the art of the poster

Graphic art, like Japanese art, was now firmly
in vogue. In 1896, Samuel Bing opened a
gallery named L'Art Nouveau, followed shortly
afterwards by his fellow German Julius Meier-
Graefe's La Maison Moderne; these exhibited
and commissioned works by Georges de Feure,
Emmanuel Orazi and others. The Exposition
Universelle of 1900 was Art Nouveau's moment
of triumph, but also signalled the start of a
decline into decadence and ornamentation.

Far removed from these
decorative excesses, the Nabis –
Bonnard, Vuillard, Ibels, Vallotton
and their friend Toulouse-Lautrec –
were working in other directions,
integrating the principles of Japanese
graphic design into Western
aesthetics. Working on the fringes
of the publishing and advertising
worlds, they unleashed one

The stiffness and
firm outlines of
Grasset's style (left)
found their antithesis
in the extravagance of
Mucha (above), who
pushed his style to ever
more elaborate heights.
He came to embody
Art Nouveau at its
most flamboyant.

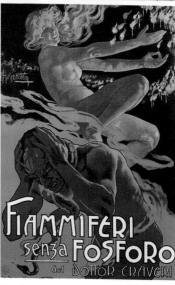

shockwave after another with their posters for the magazines *La Revue Blanche* and *La Plume*. The genius of Toulouse-Lautrec, with his brilliant layouts and use of flat colour, became hugely influential around the world.

Paris's celebration of poster art was now at its height, and the degree of artistic creativity deployed in the advertising world at this time was unsurpassed. Each artist had his own individual approach – the dozens of names include the socialist Théodore Steinlen, Jules

Paris was notable for its posters by top-flight artists, whether on an occasional basis, as with Bonnard's poster for France-Champagne (top right), or more regularly, as with professional illustrator Steinlen (top left).

Alexandre Grün, Adolphe Willette and all the denizens of Montmartre, illustrators throughout the city, and advertising pioneers such as Firmin Bouisset, creator of the Chocolat Menier girl, and O'Galop, father of the Michelin Man. Together they encouraged an appetite for beautiful advertising images that spread worldwide.

Meanwhile, in Italy, artists such as Adolfo Hohenstein, Marcello Dudovich, Giovanni Mataloni and Leopoldo Metlicovitz transformed Art Nouveau into Stile Liberty, characterized by its exuberance and richness of colour. At the opposite end of the spectrum, in the Calvinist Netherlands, Johan Thorn Prikker and Jan Toorop entered the field of graphic art under the influence of Brussels, capital of Art Nouveau.

Brussels: hub of Art Nouveau

Small in size but rich from its colonial possessions in the Congo, from its coal mines and from industry, Belgium was in the forefront of creativity, both in the artistic and the social sphere. Recognition of this fact came in the form of the Exposition Universelle staged in Brussels in 1897. Benefitting from its central geographical position, and its dissimilarity with Paris, deemed too large and frivolous, during the last decade of the 19th century Brussels became the meeting place and melting pot of all the avant-garde movements of Europe.

In 1833, a clutch of enlightened bourgeois (including Octave Maus and Edmond Picard) and outstanding artists (James Ensor, Theo van Rysselberghe, Fernand Khnopff, Victor Horta and Henry van de Velde) set up Les XX ('The Twenty'), later to become known as La Libre Esthétique. 'What I like about Les XX is their lack of a programme,' wrote Félicien Rops to Maus, and indeed over the years their number included Rodin, Seurat and Renoir alongside Chéret, the ceramicist Delaherche, the English artists Burne-Jones and Walter Crane and the Dutch Thorn Prikker, not to mention Cézanne and Gauguin. Music and literature were also strongly represented, the latter by Mallarmé among others. In line with the belief of Les XX that the fine arts and the applied arts should be treated on an equal footing, the decorative arts began to rise in status; their

In 1903, Leonetto Cappiello set the seal on advertising art's departure from realism: his green horsewoman on a red horse for Chocolat Klaus (opposite, above centre) opened the way for a long series of posters in which a figure set against a plain background became identified with a brand. The concept was embraced by other advertisers: O'Galop designed Bibendum, the Michelin Man, who is still familiar today (opposite, below left), while Chocolat Menier commissioned Bouisset to design a little girl whose design evolved over the years until the brand disappeared. Every country had its own graphic style: for instance, Italian Art Nouveau was unmistakably Latin and flamboyant, distinguished by its vivid, saturated colours and symbolic scenes featuring classically inspired figures, as demonstrated by by Adolfo Hohenstein's poster for phosphorus-free matches (opposite, below right).

belief in the social nature of Art Nouveau, meanwhile, found tangible expression in Victor Horta's Maison du Peuple (built 1896–1900).

It is therefore no surprise that Belgium followed France and experienced its own golden age of poster art and publishing in general. Privat-Livemont was the Belgian answer to Alphonse Mucha, while Victor Mignot and the heavily Japanese-influenced Constantin Meunier papered the walls of Brussels with their posters. In Liège, meanwhile, Berchmans, Donnay and Rassenfosse held sway. Art books flourished, and the same artists produced illustrations for works by Verhaeren and other Belgian authors. In 1898, in what was surely a unique alliance between Art Nouveau and the world of business and commerce, van de Velde designed what was effectively a 'house style' for the Cologne-based food manufacturer Tropon, ranging from packaging to posters and even the company letterhead. Van de Velde's style, already spare, now reflected the architect Horta's precept: 'Let's get rid of the flower and the leaf and keep the stem.' In 1895, van de Velde had himself expressed a desire to unify form and function in his designs for a house, Bloemenwerf, in which structural elements took precedence over decorative ones. But when in 1904 the industrialist Alphonse Stoclet commissioned Viennese architect and designer Josef Hoffmann to design a mansion in Brussels, the die was cast: from this moment on, Germany and Austria became the cradles of artistic invention in Europe.

Belgium was rightly seen as a capital of Art Nouveau, and the two posters reproduced here bear witness to the outstanding quality of its graphic art. This tiny country even boasted two major creative centres: Liège, where Emile Berchmans (beer poster left, before the brand name has been added) led the field, and Brussels, where Privat-Livemont, with his icy palette and white outlines (see poster for gas lamps opposite), produced variations on the style of Mucha.

Vienna: the end of ornament

Under the leadership of the architect Otto Wagner and with the painter Gustav Klimt as their guiding spirit, a whole generation of Viennese artists rejected academicism and the bourgeois decorative style – a mixture of Renaissance, baroque and rococo – that was then current. From 1894, Wagner and Joseph Maria Olbrich preached the primacy of structure over decoration. In 1897, led by Klimt, they resigned from the Künstlerhaus, the official body governing the organization of the fine arts, and became the Secession. Key figures in this movement alongside Klimt, Wagner and Olbrich included Kolo Moser and Josef Hoffmann. Klimt became president of the Secession and designed its first poster, the symbolically apt *Theseus Slaying the Minotaur*. The following year, Olbrich designed the Secession building, in which he broke with all the canons of academicism and instead created forms which he believed mirrored contemporary culture. Nothing now went unquestioned, and Hoffmann in particular could not understand how people who dressed in the latest fashions could live in buildings that had remained unchanged since the 16th century. In 1900, the Scottish architect and designer Charles Rennie Mackintosh and his wife and collaborator Margaret Macdonald were invited to Vienna for a triumphant exhibition, while the small Secession stand at the Exposition Universelle in Paris was enthusiastically received.

In 1898, the Secession launched the periodical *Ver Sacrum* (Sacred Spring), which ran until

In 1898, Henry van de Velde created a true revolution for the dried food company Tropon (opposite, below): instead of depicting their products in a realistic manner, he used a stylized version of the company's three sparrows to sell and advertise their entire range (see page 10). In a similar way, in 1893, the antiseptic firm Odol chose to use a bottle and a style of lettering that were immediately recognizable – apart from a few tweaks, the packaging remained almost unchanged for seventy years (left, the bottle of 1893; right, from 1963).

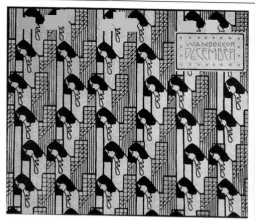

1903 and became a showcase of design. It was revolutionary in every way: the contributors were unpaid, and the editorship rotated between the founders. The square format was unprecedented, as was the choice of high-quality paper suitable for typographical experimentation. The design style tended towards the geometric and made particular use of white space to allow the pages to 'breathe'. In combination with black, this produced intriguing experiments on the notions of positive and negative, but as regards printing techniques and use of colour, anything was permitted. In short, *Ver Sacrum* was the first magazine to be devoted to graphic design.

The Secession also produced posters that contrasted sharply with both the shallow and pretentious style then prevalent and also the decorative excesses of Jugendstil. Kolo Moser and Berthold Löffler produced designs that tended towards decorative abstraction, with lettering playing a key role in the composition, while Kokoschka's work looked forward to Expressionism.

In 1903, with the financial support of the industrialist Fritz Waerndorfer, Hoffmann and Moser founded the Wiener Werkstätte (Viennese Workshops), clearly influenced by William Morris and the Arts and Crafts movement; the stripped-down geometric style of their

The Vienna Secession artists (drawing of the Secession building, opposite below) were preoccupied with structure, stylization and simplification. The heavily stylized logo of the Wiener Werkstätte (opposite above), probably designed by Kolo Moser, heralded a new graphic approach.

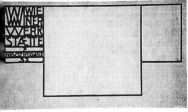

work also anticipated the Bauhaus. Alongside the many decorative objects they produced, the Wiener Werkstätte were also interested in graphic design in all its forms, including books, logos, advertising, posters and even postcards, of which they produced several series.

The presence of so many high-calibre artists ensured that Vienna became not only a teeming hive of creativity but also the capital of avant-garde movements in the applied arts. The designs reproduced in the short-lived periodical *Die Fläche* (1903–4) show the very high standard of work achieved even by lesser-known artists such as the Hagenbund (named after the café where they held their meetings), led by the talented typographer Heinrich Lefler. Egon Schiele designed a poster for the Secession in 1918, but died later that same year, as did Klimt, Wagner and Moser, against the backdrop of the crumbling Austrian empire. Vienna was never the same again.

The stylized work of the contributors to *Ver Sacrum* (such as Kolo Moser, above right and opposite) grew more and more extreme. Their imagery was innovative but became increasingly grim, depicting a world on the brink of the abyss.

Germany: a new profession

Although united by its defeat of France in 1871, Germany remained a constellation

JOSEF HOFFMANN

KOLOMAN MOSER

J. M. AUCHENTALLER

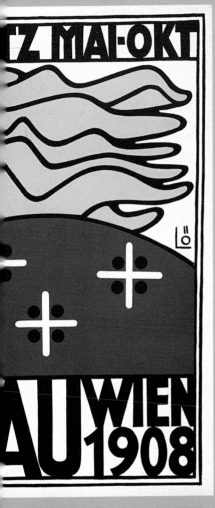

GUSTAV KLIMT

ALFRED ROLLER

RUDOLF BACHER

ADOLF BÖHM

O. SCHIMKOWITZ

The posters of the Vienna Secession, created each year by its members, were generally in a reduced, pared-down style. For their 1908 exhibition, Berthold Löffler designed an image that was fresh both in its design and in its rendering of the female form. Her dazzling colours and strong outlines make her far removed from the nymphs and Ophelias of the Pre-Raphaelites and bourgeois art.

Imported from Japan, the vogue for monograms took hold in the 1890s. The most famous example is probably Toulouse-Lautrec's 'HTL' (below), dashed onto the page with sensual flair. Viennese artists, by contrast, viewed them as exercises in seeking balance through an architectural geometry of form (left and below), as in the monogram of the Wiener Werkstätte (opposite, far left). Their rhythmic quality and faultless proportions push them to the edge of abstraction.

LEOPOLD BAUER

RUDOLF JETTMAR

ERNST STÖHR

of principalities and grand duchies orbiting around
the kingdom of Prussia. The wealthy German
bourgeoisie was no more open to art than its
Austro-Hungarian neighbours, and a stultifying
academicism, reinforced by strict censorship, stifled
any expressions of true creativity. Franz von Stuck's
poster for the Munich Secession in 1893 remained
heavily Greek-influenced in style. It was the satirical
press that offered salvation. A three-month period
in 1896 saw the launch in Munich of both *Jugend*
(which eventually gave its name to Jugendstil) and
Simplicissimus, while *Pan*, a predominantly literary
journal, had been founded the previous year in
Berlin. These three iconoclastic publications gave
rise to a form of graphic design that, although
inspired by the Parisian example, soon found its
own identity, defined by areas of flat colour, strong
outlines and bold page layouts. Their use of line
would never attain the elegance of Toulouse-Lautrec
or Steinlen, but Thomas Theodor Heine's bulldog
for *Simplicissimus* was all the more powerful for
its raw brutality. Around the Die XI Scharfrichter
('The Eleven Executioners') cabaret, Julius Diez,
Olaf Gulbransson, Bruno Paul, Hans Neumann
and Heine himself developed a joyous new form
of graphic design. Heine even managed to sell it
to a few Berlin advertisers such as Züst and Zeiss.

Germany had followed the great industrial fairs of the
19th century (particularly the Great Exhibition of 1851
in London), and in the wake of Britain's example had
opened museums devoted to the decorative arts. The
Arts and Crafts movement also influenced a handful
of initiatives such as the Vereinigte Werkstätten für
Kunst im Handwerk (United Workshops for Art in
Craftsmanship), which opened in Munich in 1897.

The revival of the applied arts

The first spark of this revival was found not in the
great cities of Berlin or Munich, sluggish and bourgeois
as they were, but in Darmstadt, due to the genuinely
enlightened influence of Grand Duke Ernst Ludwig
of Hesse, grandson of Queen Victoria. In 1899 he

The influence of the
Glasgow School is
clearly evident in this
poster by Peter Behrens
for the exhibition that
he staged in Darmstadt,
which marked
Germany's first break
from the academicism
then in vogue. Pared-
down forms, stylization
and rejection of all
ornamentation were
the guiding principles
adopted by the
Darmstadt artists'
colony in all fields.

summoned Olbrich, and soon afterwards Behrens. Olbrich set up an artists' colony around a central studio, with the aim of bringing about a revival of the applied arts: an initiative heavily influenced by the philosophy of Nietzsche ('to construct concepts, genres, laws, aims with which to make our existence possible').

Behrens's exhibition in Darmstadt in 1901, entitled 'Ein Dokument Deutscher Kunst', was very influential. He believed it essential that 'from every vital activity a gift of beauty should flow, in keeping with the spirit of the times'. This concept of the *Gesamtkunstwerk* spread rapidly following Darmstadt's success at the Exposition

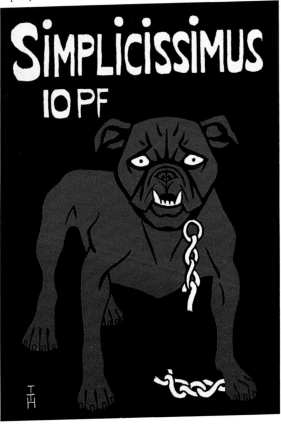

This red bulldog made a suitably uncompromising image for the launch of the magazine *Simplicissimus* by the publisher Albert Langen in Munich in 1896. Taking its inspiration from the satirical magazines produced in Paris, it brought together a talented group of angry young artists, including Bruno Paul, Olaf Gulbransson, Angelo Jank and Albert Weisgerber. The angriest of them all was Thomas Theodor Heine, who after producing this poster was dubbed the 'German Lautrec'. The image was all the more shocking in the suffocatingly bourgeois and rigidly censored climate of Munich at this time. Like the Beggarstaffs, Heine found that advertisers were reluctant to use his images, which they found far too challenging for their tastes. The exceptions were Zeiss, who commissioned a devil to advertise their inks, and the Züst automobile company, for whom the bulldog was adapted into the shape of a car radiator grill.

Universelle of 1901, where it won the gold medal for interior design. Behrens became director of the Düsseldorf School of Decorative Arts in 1903, while van de Velde was appointed to Weimar. In Berlin in 1900, meanwhile, Fritz H. Ehmcke, Kleukens and Behrens opened the Steglitz Studio, devoted to graphic art.

In 1889, the Berthold foundry created the Akzidenz Grotesk typeface, and within the space of a few years, Germany, the home of traditional, high-quality printing, saw a revolution in typography, rushing headlong from Gothic to sans serif typefaces, which were to prove eternally stylish. Behrens, Otto Eckmann, Ehmcke and a little later Lucian Bernhard all brought radical new ideas to the world of printing. In sharp contrast to William Morris, who had detested mechanization and clung to the idea of craftsmanship, German artists were convinced that art and commerce could complement one another, and therefore put their skills at the service of big business and mass production.

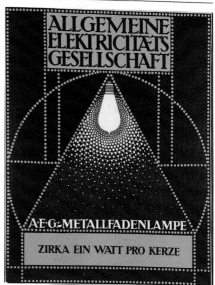

In the service of industry

The logical culmination of this was the founding of the Werkbund in 1907, in which twelve manufacturers and

Peter Behrens, a founder member of the Werkbund, collaborated with the industrialist Rathenau to produce the first all-encompassing graphic 'house style' for the AEG electric company. He designed not only their brochures and advertising material (below left) and their posters (above), but also their stores (left). The culmination of this extraordinary partnership was Behrens's architectural designs for the construction of the company's turbine hall in Berlin; an exceptional piece of work.

Akzi.iDeNZ

twelve designers joined forces to analyse the problems of production and their relationship with the consumer. The key figure in this initiative was Hermann Muthesius, who had been responsible for importing the first innovative ideas from Britain. Muthesius was a fervent advocate of standardization as a means of improving the basic product: the Werkbund exhbition in Cologne in 1914 became the culmination of these ideas. Among the members of the Werkbund were Peter Behrens and Emil Rathenau, head of the electrical manufacturing corporation AEG (and dubbed its 'chief executive artist'). The collaboration between the two produced the first truly integral use of design within industry: Behrens designed products, advertising images and stores for AEG and, in 1908, even a glass-and-steel factory.

In 1902, Karl Ernst Osthaus founded the Folkwang Museum in Essen, employing Behrens and van de Velde as architects. In parallel with this, he founded a museum in Hagen devoted to art in business and industry, complete with an archive and a system of evaluating the efficacy of advertising posters. In 1911, he published six pioneering monographs devoted to poster artists and staged the first exhibition on the theme of art in the service of industry.

In under a decade, graphic art in Germany had undergone a complete transformation. Although both puritanism and awkward regulations prohibited the use of large formats, Germany had nevertheless witnessed the birth of its own poster art. Under director Ernst Growald, the Berlin printers Hollerbaum & Schmidt brought together a galaxy of talented artists. Foremost

In 1889, the German type foundry Berthold created the Akzidenz Grotesk typeface. At a time when typography was engulfed in the arabesques of Art Nouveau, it was a watershed moment, and became the first sans serif face to enjoy widespread success.

For the Werkbund exhibition of 1914, which showcased the developing links between industrialists and designers, Fritz Ehmcke stayed true to the classical approach to typography that he pursued for the rest of his life. His restrained poster design (above) accurately reflects the rigour of the Werkbund's approach.

among them was the cartoonist and humorist Julius Klinger, who also proved a wildly inventive graphic designer. He was followed by Lucian Bernhard, who invented the *Sachplakat*, a form of poster in which the goods for sale were depicted on a large scale and accompanied by uncompromising typography. Bernhard created entirely visual campaigns for the cigarette company Manoli, and the typefaces he designed (notably Block in 1912) set new industry standards. Hans Rudi Erdt and Julius Gipkens followed in his footsteps, while Ernst Deutsch captured graphically the decadence of fashionable places of entertainment, and Paul Scheurich depicted the placid pastimes of the middle classes.

Between 1905 and the start of the First World War, Berlin produced a wealth of high-quality advertising designs. Julius Klinger often used animals (tie ad with toucan, left), following Cappiello's work in Paris. However, while Cappiello used pastels to produce a fine-art rendering, Klinger's treatment was strictly graphic.

Munich received its own wake-up call from an undisputed master of the art, Ludwig Hohlwein. Perhaps inspired by the work of the Beggarstaffs in London, this prodigiously talented designer made great use of areas of flat colour and plays on light and shade. He turned his skills to every aspect of graphic design, from beer mugs to posters, with apparently effortless ease. Also working in Munich were a group of artists known as 'The Six': Franz Paul Glass, Fritz Heubner, Carl Moos, Emil Praetorius, Max Schwarzer and Valentin

Zietara. Worthy rivals to their colleagues in Berlin, all these artists rose to prominence, being promoted with typical efficiency.

In 1905, Dr Hans Sachs was the moving spirit behind the Verein der Plakatfreunde (Society of Friends of the Poster), which in 1910 launched *Das Plakat* ('The Poster'), one of the more enduring of the many, often short-lived, publications launched throughout Europe, and especially in Paris, during this period.

In the field of book publishing, Leipzig, with its strong tradition of printing and publishing, staged a huge exhibition, directed by Walter Tiemann (founder of the Janus Press), entitled 'Bugra' (Books and Graphic Arts). It became the unrivalled commercial forum for the

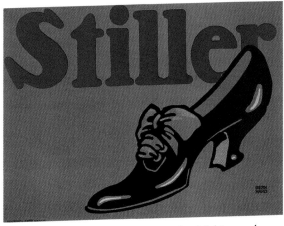

graphic arts. Indeed, in all aspects of publishing and printing, Germany in 1914 was at the cutting edge.

While Britain had failed to establish a working dialogue between the realism of the Arts and Crafts movement and the conservatism of industrialists and manufacturers, and while France had focused on single, luxury items and an elitist form of decorative art, Germany was alone in Europe in successfully creating a modern vision of art. Across the Atlantic, meanwhile, America too was making the first steps towards a different but equally effective way of working.

Lucian Bernhard's prize-winning poster for Priester matches opened the way to a new kind of advertising image. The *Sachplakat* ('object-poster') had no superfluous decorative elements or storyline, and eschewed all slogans, explanatory texts and blurbs. On a plain ground, all attention was focused on the object itself, generally depicted in a flat, minimalist style. The brand name was included in large characters, but no extraneous elements were allowed to compromise the strict purity of the object-brand relationship. The Stiller shoes poster (left) was the first in a long line for Bernhard, who went on to create advertising for Adler typewriters, Steinway pianos, Café Hag coffee and Manoli cigarettes. His work for Manoli, with its minimalist logo and stylistic variations (opposite, top and bottom), was exemplary. The *Sachplakat* became a major feature of German advertising, used by Hans Rudi Erdt for Ita Ci Fa cigars and by Julius Gipkens for Brickett Kaiser and Continental tyres.

The United States: modern times

Although the United States at the end of the Civil War was already an economic power of considerable consequence, in the fields of culture and the arts it was virgin territory. Large printing firms such as Strobridge, Forbes and Courrier made large-format posters perfectly suited to the oversized scale favoured by entrepreneurs such as P. T. Barnum, but employed stolidly conservative designers to produce works in which realism vied with plain vulgarity. The Chicago World's Fair of 1893 ushered in a new spirit of openness, which was fostered by magazine publishers. Following the example of Harper and Brothers, which by 1860 had become the world's largest publisher of newspapers and magazines, America now looked to Paris, with Louis J. Rhead producing highly artistic posters influenced by Grasset, while J. J. Gould designed covers for *Lippincott's*, and Maxfield Parrish for *The Century*. But the most talented artist of all was Will Bradley, who was influenced by Beardsley and the tenets of the Arts and Crafts movement. The success of his designs for *The Inland*

Will Bradley was one of the most outstanding of all Art Nouveau artists, hailed by critic Octave Uzanne as 'the most startling and perhaps the strongest of all poster artists in America'. Using Caslon Old Type fonts and woodcut techniques, his style became known as the '*Chap Book* style', after the magazine for which he designed his first posters (above left and right). In his long career he designed type for the American Type Founders Company, and was art director for *Collier's* magazine before becoming responsible for all Hearst Group publications.

Printer and *The Chap Book* and his posters for Victor Cycles encouraged him to set up his own company (Wayside Press); under its auspices, in the spirit of William Morris, he developed his typographical skills in the periodical *Bradley: His Book.*

RICH Spirits

While America had touched upon the Art Nouveau arena with the work of artists such as these and the glass manufacturer Tiffany, in other fields it played a more pioneering role. In 1860, over five thousand magazines were published in the United States, the most successful of them soon including up to one hundred pages of advertisements – a commercial windfall which by 1900 generated the colossal sum of $95 million. Specialized agencies – the forerunners of modern ad agencies – swiftly took over the organization of advertising space. Equally swiftly, these agencies began to take an interest in the creative side of advertising, and in 1891 Ayer and Co. became the first agency to open an art department.

There were so many new titles that competition was cut-throat and costs were pared down: the invention of Linotype meant that the workforce could be slashed to one eighth of its former size. New typefaces were created: in 1894, Linn Boyd Benton designed Century, and two years later Goudy created Camelot – the first of 199 typefaces in his career. The technological advances created by American printers are indisputable. Meanwhile, faithful to the America's fabled worship of size, Henry John Heinz acquired a six-storey site in New York and emblazoned it with a 44-foot-long pickle.

From handbills for magazines (above left) to huge billboards, America soon became the world's most prolific consumer of advertising. The need for legibility and novelty led to the rise of typographers such as Frederic W. Goudy (Goudy Old Style typeface, above), Morris Fuller Benton, Oswald Cooper and William Dwiggins. Below, Heinz billboard, New York, 19th century.

Within a triangle formed by Moscow, Berlin and Amsterdam, with Dada artists and Constructivists as their leading players and De Stijl and the Bauhaus as their meeting places, the avant-garde movements of Europe threw away the rule book and – using photography and new forms of typography as their tools – invented modern graphic design.

CHAPTER 2

REVOLUTIONS AND AVANT-GARDES

As a Bauhaus student from 1923, Joost Schmidt was taught by László Moholy-Nagy. In the same year, he designed his first poster (opposite), following his tutor's rules of asymmetry. The influence of the Bauhaus spread throughout central Europe in the 1930s, as seen in this Gillette advertisement (right) by József Pécsi, a photographer from Hungary.

The slaughter of the Great War had left Europe weak, drained and bankrupt. If there was one thing the warring nations had learned, it was the importance of communication, whether to raise funds or to sustain morale among the civilian population. The best graphic artists were mobilized, but to little avail. The most brilliant exception came in 1916 with Alfred Leete's 'Your country needs YOU', inscribed beneath Lord Kitchener's accusing finger, which was adapted to include an image of Uncle Sam by James Montgomery Flagg the following year. It was in the neutral countries of Europe – Switzerland, the Netherlands and post-Revolutionary Russia – that the future was being shaped.

Freedom for all

The rise of Cubism is too frequently and inaccurately associated with the development of graphic design. Admittedly, Braque and Picasso's collages of 1911 and 1912 partly opened the way to the technique of montage, but there was little direct influence. The Futurist movement, however, had lit the powder keg before the outbreak of war. Their first manifesto, which appeared on the front page of *Le Figaro* on 20 February 1909, was a genuine revolution. Their slogan, 'le mots en liberté' (freedom for words), called every aspect of typography into question. In everything they did, the Futurists understood the importance of publicity, from massive leafleting campaigns and use of the media to fly-posters in Italy bearing the word *Futurismo* in red on a white background. This approach was as firmly in the spirit of advertising as it was in the spirit of Futurism, which demanded a universally applicable aesthetic and rejected all hierarchical distinctions between fine art and applied art. It was in the same liberating spirit that in 1917 French poet Guillaume Apollinaire, having suggested that the poetry of the age could be found in posters and advertisements, published his *Calligrammes*, offering a similarly experimental approach to typography and the relationship between words and images.

YOUR COUNTRY NEEDS "YOU"

Some images become icons, and one of the most famous examples is Alfred Leete's 'Your Country Needs YOU' (below), created in 1914 and adapted and subverted by pacifists ever since. In 1971, the 'Committee to Help Unsell the War', comprising over thirty advertising agencies, produced an anti-Vietnam War version featuring Uncle Sam, wounded and in tatters, above the words 'I Want OUT'. In 1991, Stephen Kroninger opposed the Gulf War with a poster of a misshapen George Bush with the slogan 'Uncle George Wants You..'; and in 2003 George W. Bush made a similar appearance on a Micah Wright poster opposing the war in Iraq.

Typographical games are nothing new: a printer named Pélissier, for example, set the text of Marie-Antoinette's last letter in lines of unequal length to form the shape of the queen's profile, while Lewis Carroll and Stéphane Mallarmé were among the first to overturn the established rules of typography in books. Guillaume Apollinaire formalized these experiments in the poems of *Calligrammes* (1917), in which the arrangement of the type echoed the meaning of the words (above left). The Dadaists and Futurists went even further, pushing type to extremes in their many leaflets and manifestos.

In 1916, at the Cabaret Voltaire in Zurich, Tristan Tzara, Hugo Ball, Hans Richter and Jean Arp responded to the horrors of the war by questioning all the values of Western culture. Contemptuous, provocative, scathing and destructive, the movement they founded – Dada – spread through Europe and to America after the war, with its main centres in Paris, Berlin and New York. Dada pamphlets and posters were naturally iconoclastic in their typography, while their collages and montages were adopted by avant-garde movements everywhere.

De Stijl, a universal vision

De Stijl came into being in the Netherlands, another neutral country, between 1915 and 1917. The architect

H. P. Berlage had already prepared the ground, and Bart van de Leck's geometric poster design for the Rotterdam–London steamer line in 1916 anticipated the rigour of the De Stijl movement. Theo van Doesburg founded the magazine *De Stijl* along with Vilmos Huszár (who designed the cover typography), J. J. P. Oud, Bart van der Leck and Piet Mondrian; it ran from 1918 until 1931. In a protest against the war,

individualism and nationalism, De Stijl sought to create a universal vision that was Calvinist in its austerity. De Stijl artists organized space on geometric principles and used only pure colour, proposing a new and universal concept of art that rose above the specifics of appearance, naturalistic forms and colours. Going to the opposite extreme, they found their means of expression in the abstraction of form and colour, and in the use of straight lines and blocks of primary colour. Their most striking creations were in the field of architecture; the Café de Unie in Rotterdam and L'Aubette in Strasbourg. Graphically, the magazine

Architects played a dominant part in the Dutch avant-garde: the two most influential magazines, *De Stijl* (left) and *Wendingen* (above), were laid out with rigorous restraint, using the rectangle as their basic unit. Werkman, from the world of traditional printing, was one exception to this rule (below).

favoured sans serif typefaces and the use of the square as the basic unit for page layouts that became ever more purist and minimalist.

In the same year, 1918, Hendrik T. Wijdeweld, another architect, founded a magazine on the visual arts, entitled *Wendingen* (Changes). Until 1927, Wijdeweld was both its publisher and its designer, choosing an unusual square format and using sans serif faces on rare Chinese paper, which he bound with raffia in heavily Japanese-inspired fashion. Unlike *De Stijl*, *Wendingen* was eclectic in style, varying its cover art in accordance with the contents of each issue.

Also in the Netherlands, between 1923 and 1926 Hendrik N. Werkman used his small printing workshop to produce a magazine entitled *The Next Call*, in which he gave free rein to all forms of experimentation, from wood type to *objets trouvés*, from Dada to abstraction. Working on the fringes of the main currents in art at the time, he established his own profoundly personal and radical style.

The Russian avant-garde

Revolutionary artists in Russia enjoyed the exhilarating experience of using their skills to further the revolution through which they were living. It was in 1915, however, well before those three weeks in 1917 that shook the world, that Kasimir Malevich exhibited his black square on a white ground and so invented Suprematism. Earlier still, in 1912, a group of artists centred on Vladimir Mayakovksy had issued a manifesto entitled *A Slap in the Face of Public Taste*, which became the point of departure for Russian Futurism. In April 1918, Lenin launched street art as a form of propaganda, unleashing a creative

In September 1922, Theo van Doesburg held a Constructivist congress in Weimar, perhaps with the idea of challenging the Bauhaus on its home ground. Revealing a degree of equivocation, he also invited the leading lights of Dada, with Tzara and Arp at their head. According to Moholy-Nagy's account, the congress rapidly turned into a Dada spectacle. In the photo, Tzara kisses the hand of Nelly van Doesburg. Theo van Doesburg stands in the centre, dressed in white

with a paper hat, with Lissitzky to his right, wearing a cap. Arp stands in front at the extreme right, while Moholy-Nagy stands at the back.

explosion of form and colour of which the 'Rosta Windows' remain the most celebrated example. These graphic patriotic bulletins, posted mostly in empty shop windows, were the work of artists including Mayakovsky, Ivan Malyutin, Vladimir Lebedev and Vladimir Kozlinsky. But the fledgling USSR now found itself in desperate straits, with the young Red Army forced to defend it on all sides. With his poster of 1920 showing a red wedge slashing into the heart of a white circle, El Lissitzky produced a symbolic totem of the conflict.

The Vkhutemas art school, set up that same year in a former Fabergé factory in Moscow, was a major advance, serving as a training ground and teaching laboratory for artists; here, in a ferment of creativity that continued day and night and embraced all the decorative arts, the death of art was proclaimed.

With the New Economic Policy (NEP), the Revolution paused to draw breath and the USSR reopened trade links with the world outside. Mayakovsky set up the MAF publishing company and the magazine *Lef*, which distanced itself from Constructivism in order to assert the primacy of colour. In his essay 'The Topography of Typography', Lissitzky laid the foundations for a new typography, to be followed by the Agitreklama artists Varvara Stepanova, Alexei Levin, Anton Lavinsky and Alexander Rodchenko, who invented new types of sales poster to promote Russian goods. Mayakovsky also turned copywriter for the cause and produced rousing slogans.

Through this work, artists also gained the opportunity to travel and spread their graphic vision abroad, as Lissitzky went on to do throughout Europe.

Hot on the heels of the new typography came photomontage. After early experiments in a poetic, Dadaist vein, Rodchenko swiftly abandoned the new technique in favour of straight photography, leaving the field of political montage to its undisputed master, Gustav Klutsis, who produced 'Dynamic City' as early as 1919. The Five Year Plan posters he created from 1928,

After Stalin's rise to power in the USSR, Klutsis became the great purveyor of propaganda, using photomontages (below) that featured several fixed elements: an enlarged photograph of a heroic worker, the colour red (the only colour he allowed), and a diagonal composition, often using a flagpole. This was far removed from the teeming creativity of the 1920s, and from the radical

Constructivism of Lissitzky, whose 'Beat the Whites with the Red Wedge' (opposite below) was the movement's manifesto. This type of work was now deemed too elitist, as was the humour of Rodchenko and Mayakovsky (poster for baby products; opposite, above right).

Soviet Russia's contribution to the field of cinema was astounding, notably in the films of Eisenstein. The posters produced to publicize the films were no less striking: Lavinsky, Prusakov and particularly the Stenberg brothers (left, poster for *The Man with the Movie Camera* by Dziga Vertov, 1929) all found radical and deliriously creative new approaches. Using dizzying perspectives, découpage and collage, distortions and quasi-cinematic use of colour, they created a body of innovative work that has never been surpassed.

with their teeming masses and fervent energy, remain unparalleled. However, with the advent of Stalinism, avant-garde experimentation was frowned upon.

In the field of cinema, meanwhile, the Stenberg brothers, Gyorgy and Vladimir, created posters that were startlingly innovative, using wildly inventive colour montages that would remain unique in the history of film posters.

Bauhaus: the invention of graphic design

The First World War left Germany vanquished, drained, partly occupied and weighed down by debt (of which, in the event, very little was actually paid). To make matters worse, the new Weimar Republic was also faced with putting down the threat of Communist revolution.

But against this sombre backdrop, ideas that had first appeared before 1914 nevertheless continued to make progress. In some ways the war had created a break with the past, which worked to the advantage of modernist thinkers. The year 1919 saw the birth of the Bauhaus in Weimar and also of the Bund Deutscher Gebrauchsgraphiker (Union of German Commercial Artists).

In the wake of van de Velde, who had been working in Weimar since 1903, the Bauhaus was founded under the direction of Walter Gropius. In the beginning its work was focused around architecture, and its organization into a number of workshops meant that the movement was still heavily centred on craftsmanship. Graphic design was virtually non-existent, but the importance it attained over the years is indicative of a specifically German talent for this newly emerging discipline. In 1923, Gropius invited László Moholy-Nagy to the Bauhaus. In the two years since Moholy-Nagy had

Herbert Bayer was first a student at the Bauhaus and later a professor. His passion for graphic art in all its forms was founded on the two basic principles of simplicity and functionality (top right, poster for a Kandinsky exhibition, 1926). Both criteria are found in the Universal typeface (above), which he designed in 1926. His tutor, Moholy-Nagy, was responsible the *Bauhausbücher* series of books (top left), still the standard works of reference on Bauhaus philosophy.

moved to his Berlin studio, it had become the haunt of Kurt Schwitters, Lissitzky and van Doesburg: the same names crop up again and again in this decade of unparalleled creative innovation. Moholy-Nagy introduced the teaching of photography and typography and supervised the Bauhaus Press, through which he began to print the results of his experiments and disseminate them to a wider public.

When the Bauhaus had to move to Dessau in 1925, Moholy-Nagy opened a workshop devoted to typography and advertising art, which he entrusted to Herbert Bayer, a former student who had already, at this time of galloping inflation, designed an innovative range of banknotes for the Bank of Thuringia. At the age of 25, Bayer designed the Universal typeface, a sans serif font with no capitals. He dedicated the workshop's efforts to profit-making activities such as publishing Bauhaus books. When Bayer and Moholy-Nagy followed Gropius's example and left the Bauhaus, Bayer's successor Joost Schmidt further accentuated the pragmatic nature of its teaching. To the courses in 'advertising and printing, types of publicity and their applications as advertisements, posters and window displays' described in the prospectus for 1929 were now added the study of advertising strategies, the analysis of standard costs, and an understanding of raw materials and machinery. Walter Peterhans, in charge of photography, also concentrated on photography in advertising. Forced to leave Dessau, the Bauhaus finally moved to Berlin under the directorship of Mies van der Rohe, before being finally shut down by the Nazis.

Bayer worked not only in photography and design but in the decorative arts and architecture. His designs for exhibition stands, kiosks (below) and pavilions were three-dimensional expressions of his stringent logic, heralding a new kind of signage, restrained and colour-coded.

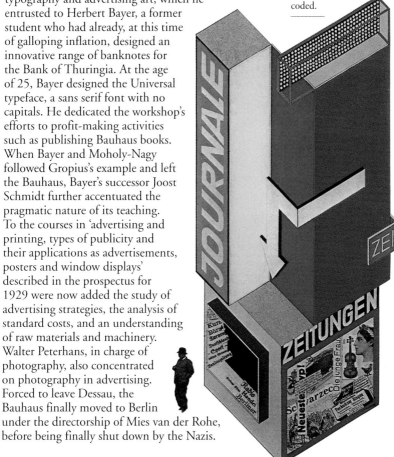

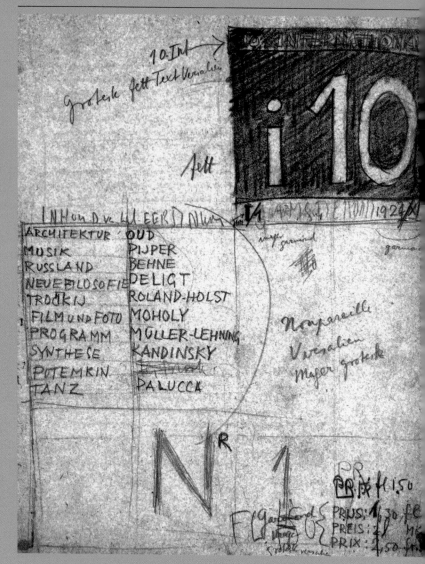

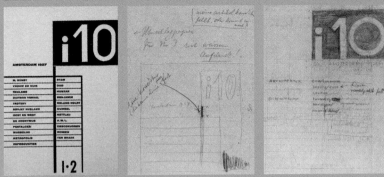

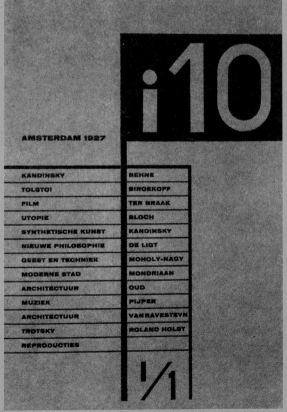

F irst published in Amsterdam in 1927 and 1928 by Arthur Lehning, the 'international revue' *i10* first appeared at around the time that *L'Esprit Nouveau*, published by Ozenfant and Le Corbusier, was – for financial reasons – fading from view, and Theo van Doesburg was producing only two or three issues of *De Stijl* annually. Co-founded with Moholy-Nagy, who worked on its design (opposite and above, sketches for the cover and title-page), the architect J. J. P. Oud and the musician Willem Pijper, *i10* made it clear from the outset that its intention was to bridge the gap between art and life, and to bring intellectual debate into the international arena.

But its ever-growing emphasis on graphic design and its use in advertising remain highly revealing of the preoccupations of the age in which it flourished.

The German example

In its own more modest fashion, and with the emphasis more on fashion and business, the Reimann School in Berlin was pushing in the same direction and developed along equally stringent lines. Its motto was 'less idealism, more application' – thus neatly summing up the paradoxes and dynamics of this period which saw the true birth of graphic design. All the leading figures in the field were outstanding creative artists working at the cutting edge of avant-garde movements, and all believed in the need to create a form of visual communication for the modern world. In 1922, van Doesburg, Lissitzky and Hans Richter convened an International Congress of Constructivists, but this did not prevent them from believing in advertising and advances in mechanization as the means to a better world.

From the late 19th century on, the Hanover firm of Pelikan inks commissioned the finest artists to design its advertising. In 1925 they hired El Lissitzky, who produced many designs for them, including an early use of photograms (above).

The year 1928 saw a key development with the formation of the Ring neuer Werbegestalter (Circle of New Artists in Advertising) on the initiative of Kurt Schwitters. The Ring numbered among its members Willy Baumeister, Walter Dexel, César Domela, Jan Tschichold, Max Burchartz, Georg Trump and the Dutch artists Piet Zwart and Paul Schuitema. They mounted exhibitions in Germany and the Netherlands, forged links with the Bauhaus, and above all worked consistently in this new discipline they were creating. At his agency, Merz Werbezentrale (Merz Advertising Centre) in Hanover, Schwitters worked for Pelikan inks and Bahlsen biscuits, as well as for the city council, for which he created a range of graphic designs between 1929 and 1932 that may have been the first in the world on such a scale. In the course of this work, he used another German innovation that eventually became generally accepted practice: the Deutsche Industrie Norm or DIN, which established standard paper formats

It was very probably due to the influence of Kurt Schwitters, who had welcomed him to Hanover in 1922, that El Lissitzky (opposite below, choosing pictures in 1928) received his first commissions from Pelikan inks. Schwitters himself worked for the firm while also, between 1923 and 1932, publishing his avant-garde magazine *Merz* (below left).

Another pioneer of photography in advertising, Max Burchartz found the Bochum steelworks to be another client, like Pelikan, that was

that were used in every area of the council's work, including transport, theatre and opera.

Max Burchartz, Johannes Canis and their agency Werbebau (Advertising Construction) carried out similar work, notably for the Bochum steelworks (where they set out to establish the 'maximum functionality') and for the city of Essen. Dexel in Jena, Baumeister in Stuttgart, Domela in Berlin, Tschichold in Munich, and Bayer who, working for the Dorland agency in Berlin, created advertisements that were startling in their novelty. Throughout Germany, prominent artists were busy

prepared to accept modernist design. He also worked for the city of Essen (above right, poster for an exhibition of advertising art, 1931).

re-inventing the graphic arts and a new approach to advertising. Lissitzky, who spent most of his working life in Germany, also worked for Pelikan: a new language was emerging.

The new typography

Typography underwent radical changes, redefined in Germany by the same key figures. 'The New Typography' by Moholy-Nagy, published by the Bauhaus in 1923; 'Topography of Typography' by El Lissitzky, published in the journal *Merz* in 1924; Schwitters's *Elementary Typography*, published in 1925; and Tschichold's *The New Typography* all wrought a radical change in the way typography was viewed.

The Futurists and Dadaists had shattered the rules that had prevailed in the 19th century; now it was time to reinvent typography in a form that was both free and functional. Lissitzky believed that typography should be an active, articulated structure echoing the dynamics of spoken language. It should also be logical. Futura, the typeface designed in 1927 by Paul Renner, became the ideal of standardized typography, as advocated by the Bauhaus. Sans serif faces became the internationally accepted norm (later rejected by the Nazis with their reintroduction of the Gothic face Fraktur), and Erbar, Trump and Schmidt all produced their own fonts.

In his preface to *The New Typography*, Jan Tschichold quoted Mondrian's words, 'We are at the turning point of civilization', and like Cendrars in his preface to

A new approach to graphic design required new typefaces. In 1927, Paul Renner designed Futura, described as 'the typeface for our times'. Ideally suited for use in photomontages, it became hugely successful. In 1930 and 1931, many type foundries launched similar typefaces: Georg Trump brought out City, Bernhard designed Bernhard Gothic and Heinrich Jost launched Beton. Used in combination with strictly geometric forms, as in this design for a sign by Walter Dexel,

(above) sans serif faces were a triumphant success.

Cassandre's *Le Spectacle est dans la Rue*, delivered a paean to the aeroplane, the telephone, the neon signs of New York, and a new type of hero: the engineer. Tschichold followed this with a plea for clarity, for the stripping away of all that was superfluous, and for asymmetry, a rhythmic expression of functional design. This new type was ideally suited for use alongside photos and photomontage.

Photography and photomontage

The use of photography was initiated by the same artists: Lissitzky, who introduced Zwart to the technique, and Moholy-Nagy, who developed a combination of word and image that he called Typophoto: 'Typography is communication composed of type. Photography is the visual representation of what can be optically apprehended. Typophoto is the visually most exact rendering of communication.'

This corresponds to an objective vision of graphic design and advertising that was expounded by Lissitzky and Mart Stam in the magazine *Die Reklame* in 1924. A poster should name the product, a poster should show the product. In fact this was a reprise of Lucian Bernhard's *Sachplakat* on a more radical scale, for a photograph of the product could depict it even more accurately then a drawing.

In the late 1920s Jan Tschichold – a trained typographer as well as a theoretician and academic – designed a series of posters for the Phoebus Palast cinema in Munich that broke completely with the accepted canons of the genre (above, poster for the film *Woman Without a Name*). Introduced to photography and montage by Lissitzky and Moholy-Nagy, he used both techniques to dazzling effect.

The contribution of these theoreticians should not be reduced to mere principles, however, for their work was underpinned by an approach to their art that was as rich as it was carefully considered. Moholy-Nagy, who was experimenting with photograms at the same time as Man Ray was inventing the rayogram, wrote at length on the relationship between light and shade, and put his findings into practice in his work. Used in this way, the photogram provided a spur to creativity in inventive ways that indicated that the spirit of Dada was not yet dead.

In 1931, at the instigation of the Ring neuer Werbegestalter, Domela staged an international exhibition of photomontage, which now spread to a huge range of creative fields. The exhibition included montages that were pure Dada in spirit by John Heartfield (notably for the magazine *AIZ*), who steadfastly held to his political militancy: 'New political problems demand new means of propaganda. For this task photography possesses the greatest power of persuasion.' Alongside these were the poetic Soviet photomontages by Klutsis; and a demonstration of photomontage in advertising, complete with impeccable typography and photography, which prompted Herbert Bayer, on leaving the exhibition, to rail against the 'Bauhaus style' – even though his own publications had been largely responsible for promoting it. 'Pure' photography, to which Rodchenko now turned and which was also the favoured medium of Burchartz, Mart Stam and Lissitzky, spread just as rapidly.

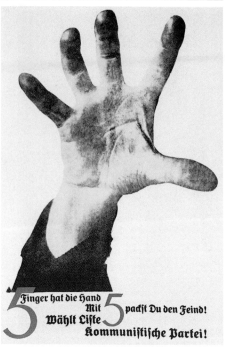

Photomontage made the most provocative associations and striking simplifications possible. The undisputed master of the technique was John Heartfield, especially with his covers for the *AIZ (Arbeiter International Zeitung)*. He also used simple photography, as in this symbolically powerful call for Communist votes (above).

The German influence

Germany not only had a talent for innovation; it was also skilled at publicizing and marketing that creative flair.

Gebrauchsgraphik, a magazine founded by the academic H. K. Frenzel, in 1928 became the official mouthpiece of the Bund Deutscher Gebrauchsgraphiker, and so kept abreast of international artistic developments. It inspired many imitators, establishing links with the rest of the world and particularly with the United States. In 1929 Frenzel, who was the guiding force behind this movement, organized a World Advertising Congress in Berlin, while Heinz and Bodo Rasch's book *Gefesselter Blick* (1930) was a comprehensive artistic inventory of the German advertising industry at this time.

The previous year, Cologne had hosted 'Pressa',

INTERNATIONALE AUSSTELLUNG
DES DEUTSCHEN WERKBUNDS

FILM
UND
FOTO

BERLIN 1929
FOTO-AUSSTELLUNG VOM 19. OKT. BIS 17. NOV.
FILM-SONDERVORFÜHRUNGEN VOM 19. OKT. BIS 19. NOV.

a massive exhibition devoted to every aspect of book publishing. While the 1925 Exposition Internationale des Arts Décoratifs in Paris had represented the heights of extravagant luxury and bourgeois taste, Pressa flung open the doors to modernism. Its pavilions were designed by the greatest architects of the time, including Erich Mendelsohn; and the photographic fresco designed

In 1928, the 'Pressa' exhibition in Cologne was a triumph (above, entrance hall and press stand). Lissitzky's interior design for the Russian pavilion, a series of photomontages in red and white, may have been his masterpiece. The following year the Werkbund's 'Film und Foto' exhibition (poster, below left) confirmed Germany's pre-eminent position in the fields of graphic art and printing.

by Lissitzky for the Russian pavilion has probably never been equalled, let alone surpassed.

When Hitler came to power the Bauhaus was forced to shut its doors, and the diaspora that followed rapidly took the German pioneers to America (Gropius and Moholy-Nagy), Switzerland (Tschichold and Max Bill) and Britain (Zero and Allner). The journal *Gebrauchsgraphik* survived, surprisingly, and Bayer

Carried by the avant-garde, the design revolution spread throughout Europe. While the principles remained constant, each movement interpreted them in its own way. One example was the inspired Futurism of Fortunato Depero, whose book *Depero Futurista* (left), with its metal cover bound with nuts and bolts and its deliriously inventive typography, has become an icon of modernism. Likewise, the witty typography of Piet Zwart (below, ad for the cable manufacturer NKF) and the dynamism of Schuitema (opposite below, brochure for Berkel scales) were both bids for freedom from a system that threatened to trap many young graphic artists.

remained in Germany until 1938, working for Dorland, notably on covers for *Neue Linie*.

From Berlin to Milan

Within a decade, Berlin had become both the focus and the mould for a style which now spread with great rapidity. The European avant-garde was highly mobile, and the times were favourable: in the turmoil that was the aftermath of the war, both Eastern and Western Europe were open to this constructive dialogue. Away from the conceptualist rigour of De Stijl, the Dutch were inspired, in the work of Piet Zwart and Paul Schuitema, to find new forms of advertising that were modern and objective. Zwart, who was close to De Stijl and worked as an assistant to the architect H. P. Berlage, described himself as a *typotekt*, both a typographer and an

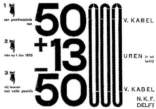

architect. In the late 1920s he worked for the Dutch post office, producing revolutionary postage stamp designs. His colleague Paul Schuitema, meanwhile, combined photography with new forms of typography. During the 1920s he worked for Berkel scales, where he combined the credo of De Stijl with the principles of Constructivism.

It was natural that the influence of the Moscow–Berlin axis should spread throughout central Europe, with its proliferation of avant-garde movements. In Poland, Futurism and Dada both found fertile ground, and the ubiquitous Lissitzky put Henryk Berlewi in contact with Berlin: in 1924 he published the manifesto *Mechano-Faktura*, and put his ideas into practice at his advertising agency, Mechano Reklama. Czechoslovakia was also at the forefront, with Ladislav Sutnar, Karel Teige, Frantisek Zelenka and many others making Prague a hotbed of modernism. Photography and the new typography were triumphant. Even in less progressive Hungary, new work by artists such as József Pécsi showed just how far avant-garde principles had spread.

Karel Teige in Czechoslovakia (above left, book on the theory of typography) and Henryk Berlewi in Poland, who experimented with Dadaist-style type (above, brochure for his agency), were both perfectionists, but neither were immune from the strictures of Structuralism.

One last unusual example deserves mention: the Futurism of Fortunato Depero. In 1931, his *Manifesto dell'arte pubblicitaria* set out his aims: 'Although when I paint pictures my inspiration is freely drawn, I use my imagination to magnify the products of Italian industry, and I do this with the same harmony of style and as much love, enthusiasm and care.' This was in the spirit of the Futurist credo, drawing no distinction between fine art and applied art. His main client was Campari, for whom he developed variations on simple images in bright colours. He also went to New York, where he produced cover art for *Harper's Bazaar* and designed advertising stands that anticipated pop art.

NE LE RENDS PAS ILLISIBLE NE LE
RENDS PAS ILLISIBLE NE LE RENDS
PAS ILLISIBLE NE LE RENDS PAS I
LLISIBLE NE LE RENDS PAS ILLISIBLE
NE LE RENDS PAS ILLISIBLE NE LE
RENDS PAS ILLISIBLE NE LE RENDS
PAS ILLISIBLE NE LE RENDS PAS I
LLISIBLE NE LE RENDS PAS ILLISIBLE
NE LE RENDS PAS ILLISIBLE NE LE
RENDS PAS ILLISIBLE NE LE RENDS
PAS ILLISIBLE NE LE RENDS PAS I
LLISIBLE NE LE RENDS PAS ILLISIBLE
NE LE RENDS PAS ILLISIBLE NE LE
RENDS PAS ILLISIBLE NE LE RENDS
PAS ILLISIBLE NE LE RENDS PAS I
LLISIBLE NE LE RENDS PAS ILLISIBLE
NE LE RENDS PAS ILLISIBLE NE LE
RENDS PAS ILLISIBLE NE LE RENDS
PAS ILLISIBLE NE LE RENDS PAS I
LLISIBLE NE LE RENDS PAS ILLISIBLE
NE LE RENDS PAS ILLISIBLE NE LE
RENDS PAS ILLISIBLE NE LE RENDS
PAS ILLISIBLE NE LE RENDS PAS I
LLISIBLE NE LE RENDS PAS ILLISIBLE

Away from the avant-garde, though not immune to its influence, creative artists in many countries continued to push down the boundaries of communications and graphic design. Stylization, simplification and a new approach to typography were the foundations of the far-reaching movement that we know today as Art Deco.

CHAPTER 3

MODERNISM TRIUMPHANT

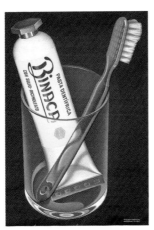

The typeface Bifur, designed by Cassandre (opposite), and the new Swiss objectivity – of which Stoecklin's Binaca poster (left) was a fine example – showed that the strict rules of the avant-garde were not the only means of progress in graphic design. Adapting their work to fit the criteria of the majority of advertisers, designers put forward their own approaches to modernism.

France: emphasis on the fine arts

In France, the 1925 Exposition Internationale des Arts Décoratifs set a tone of relentlessly 'good' taste. Pressure applied by politicians and chambers of commerce alike ensured the triumph of bourgeois art and pastiche. French modernists took refuge in the Esprit Nouveau (New Spirit) pavilion, which caused a scandal and almost did not open. Built by Le Corbusier and Pierre Jeanneret, with concrete trees by Robert Mallet-Stevens outside and Cubist paintings inside, it was furnished by René Herbst and Charlotte Perriand, two of the few modernist artists working in France. While German creative artists were supported by industrialists through the Werkbund, France remained a hostile environment. In 1929, the marginalized artists of the French avant-garde, including Jean Carlu, A. M. Cassandre, Paul Colin, Charles Loupot and Francis Bernard, united forces to form the Union des Artistes Modernes (UAM).

Paris, scene of the rise of the Ballets Russes and Cubism, home to the writers' and artists' coteries

of Montparnasse, remained the cradle of fine art: nobody here proclaimed the death of art. The Surrealists were not like the Dadaists of Berlin: here all artistic activity, including graphic design and advertising art, was rooted in the fine arts. Here there were no collective manifestos but rather the expression of individual talents, described by Carlu as 'a torrent of colour, though not without discipline': here was a

Unlike the German Werkbund, the Union des Artistes Modernes (UAM) in France received virtually no support from its nation's industrialists. However, it staged regular exhibitions at the Musée des Arts Décoratifs from 1930 onwards. Jean Carlu, a lone militant among its graphic designers, designed the poster for the third show in 1932 (above), using the geometric forms – sphere, cylinder, cone and rectangular prism – adopted as the UAM symbols. He also placed the UAM logo, designed by Pierre Legrain in 1929, at the entrance to the show (left).

warmth that stood in opposition to the chill of the avant-garde.

In France, poster artists, or *affichistes*, made their first appearance. Early in the 20th century, Leonetto Cappiello had begun to produce designs featuring figures or animals (such as the Thermogène fire-eater or the Cinzano zebra) on a plain ground, and through regular use, these came to be associated with the brand name. Legibility was his prime concern, both in the lettering and the colours he used, and this allowed him to push advertising art forward and influence a whole generation of artists, many of whom, such as Jean d'Ylen, would remain almost slavish imitators. Those who managed

to free themselves from his influence, by contrast, became the pioneers of the modern poster.

Poster pioneers

Cassandre was unquestionably the most influential *affichiste* of his generation. Influenced in his early work by Fernand Léger and Amédée Ozenfant, he nevertheless drew a clear line between his own work and Cubism: 'Some people have described my posters as Cubist: in the sense that my approach is essentially geometric and monumental, they are.' But he himself felt a closer affinity with architecture, 'the art I prefer to all others'.

While his early work was massively influential to the 'Cassandre generation', in the 1930s Leonetto Cappiello pared his style down to the essentials. His best posters from this period easily bear comparison with those of his younger colleagues.

•In his work for Kub, Cappiello shows what Hugo would have called the "stock cube effect" by going back to the "basic bull", but focusing on the head alone, depicting it as massive and magical, like a trophy displayed at a colonial exhibition. It is through this kind of elliptical regeneration that Cappiello manages to remain so modern; one of the most youthful poets working in our streets and open spaces.•
Pierre Gueguen, *Arts et Métiers Graphiques*, 15 January 1934

Cassandre combined Synthetism and lyricism to create a new form of image to exalt the product: *L'Intransigeant* was a paean to communications; *Etoile du Nord* and *Nord Express* to the railways; and *Normandie* to the great ocean liners. Master of the airbrush (a technique that enabled him to produce smooth gradations of colour), the use of perspective and layouts of breathtaking

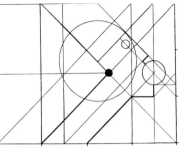

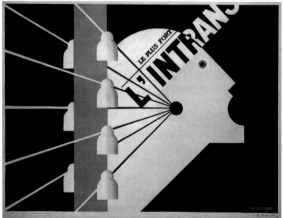

Cassandre adopted the principles of Le Corbusier – 'a module measures and unifies; a regulating line constructs and satisfies' – and applied them to his 1925 poster for *L'Intransigeant*, (left; sketch showing its composition above, published in the magazine of the Union de l'Affiche Française, December 1926).

It was this rigour that attracted Cassandre to typography (sample of

Le PEIGNOT A ÉTÉ GRAVÉ SUR bois POUR AFFI-CHES, EN GRAS ET demi-GRAS dE 6 À 40 cicÉROS. Il EST EMPLOYÉ AUSSI POUR LA TYPOGRAPHIE MURALE, EN LETTRES bois ET CARTON dÉCOUPÉS.

audacity, he produced a body of work – with a few rare exceptions – of extraordinary power. His secret, the element that made him an artist in the purest subjective tradition, was, in his own words, his belief that, because advertising had 'to speak to everyone, and to do it quickly, it has only one chance of making itself heard, and that is the language of poetry.'

Peignot typeface, above) and also let him use his innate understanding of graphic progression to design his iconic triptych for Dubonnet (opposite, below).

He was also able to move away from objects and machines and invent new characters, such as the Dubonnet man, or to reinvent existing ones, as in his poster for Nicolas, which anticipated kinetic art. Showing the osmosis between French painting and advertising, from 1935 his work displayed more fluid lines, revealing the influence of Surrealism.

Cassandre was also France's only truly revolutionary typographer. Very early in his career he declared his preference for 'the pure product of the ruler and compass', and his belief that 'the design should revolve around the text, and not vice versa'. In 1929, he designed the Bifur typeface for the Deberny & Peignot foundry, who presented it to the public in the following terms: 'Neither we nor Cassandre have sought to create something "pretty". We have set out to create a typeface for advertising, stripping every character of all that is not strictly necessary to distinguish it from the rest.' This functionalist typeface, 'designed to be a metaphorical broom or an internal combustion engine', caused an uproar, and the fonts Acier Noir (1936) and Peignot (1937) soon followed. Cassandre also used photography (for Pernod) and photomontage

●A contemporary document, the sketch for *L'Intransigeant*, sheds light on Cassandre's method of composition. It consists of a rectangle, its base divided into four modules and its sides into three. The composition is constructed on two squares of three modules, overlapping by two-thirds, and is governed by the right angles formed by their sides and their diagonals...the geometry of this composition is so pronounced that it goes beyond the idea of regulating lines: the geometry dictates the form.●

Henri Mouron
(above, Cassandre in his studio, *c.* 1935

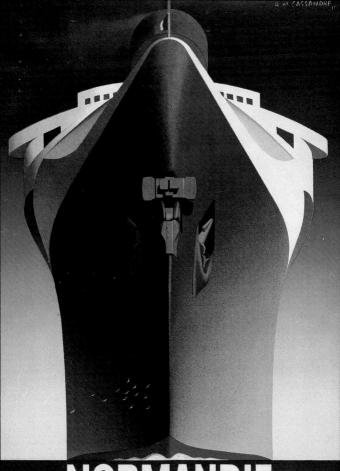

CHEMIN DE FER DU NORD

A.M.CASSANDRE 27

SOCIÉTE NATIONALE DES CHEMINS DE FER BELGES

NEDERLANDSCHE SPOORWEGEN

ÉTOILE DU NORD

DU DÉJEUNER PULLMAN AU DINER

PARIS — BRUXELLES — AMSTERDAM

COMPAGNIE DES WAGONS-LITS

VICTOIRE!

A 2 DOIG

Cassandre's posters for the *Etoile du Nord* (1927; above left) and the *Normandie* (1935; opposite) are striking examples of his talent for inventing new and powerful images. Though designed seven years apart, they display the same conceptual rigour, and the same use of perspective and steep viewing angles. In the geometric *Etoile du Nord*, the rails converge on a vanishing point placed at the top of the image, with just enough space above to show a narrow strip of sky and the eponymous star. In the *Normandie* poster the effect is reversed: the prow of the steamer, seen from below and disproportionately large, occupies the upper part of the composition, leaving only a narrow band at the bottom for the sea. In both cases the effect is striking and impossible to ignore. In Cassandre's work, rigour never froze into rigidity, however. His virtuoso skill at airbrushing breathed a vibrant sensuality into these massive machines, while the typography never compromises the purity of the image. The type is an extension of the ship's hull in the *Normandie*, while in the *Etoile du Nord* it runs right around the outer edge. He was also skilled at photomontage (below left, Triplex brochure).

(his brochure for Triplex glass). It was with some justification that he wrote: 'The language of advertising has been born: only just, but it has been born.'

Charles Loupot – with whom Cassandre had worked at the Alliance Graphique agency – also favoured geometric compositions but with a more delicate approach, using vibrant lithography and warmer colours combined with harmonious lettering. His posters for Twinings and Café Martin are still lifes of potent serenity. Following the example of Cassandre, he created Cubist-inspired figures (for Galeries Barbès and Valentine) and produced more stylized versions of others, such as the character of Nectar the delivery man for the wine merchants

Nicolas, and most famously the two waiters of the aperitif St Raphaël, whom, over a period of twenty years, he pushed ever further towards abstraction. His poster for Coty, meanwhile, is a Surrealist-inspired vision.

Jean Carlu owed a considerable debt to the painter Juan Gris, and built his early posters (for Gellé and Monsavon) around the use of flat planes. Adopting a strictly geometric approach in his work for the Théâtre Pigalle, he also used photography and photomontage (as in his posters 'La dette' and 'Pour la paix'). He took a leading role in the struggles of the UAM, and was heavily involved in events such as their 1937 exhibition.

Bringing up the rear of this pioneering group, Paul Colin was a painterly *affichiste*, most of whose work was for theatres and music halls, including the design of

Following the example of Cappiello, who drew small preparatory sketches to find what he called the 'arabesque', Loupot covered the pages of his sketchbooks with doodles (above right). In this way, he produced increasingly stylized renditions of the two waiters serving the aperitif St Raphaël; from being shown in profile in 1937, they turned over the years to face forwards and became ever more geometric in style (above left, 1945). The culmination of this process, in the 1950s, verges on abstraction, playing on the famous black, white and red branding colours.

In addition to Loupot, the UAM had three other members who shared the same principles as Cassandre: Carlu, who used Cubist principles in his poster for Monsavon (1925; opposite, below left); Paul Colin, who revolutionized theatre and music-hall posters – at this period still close to illustration – with his Revue Nègre poster (1925; opposite, below right); and the unjustly neglected Francis Bernard, who produced a conceptual image of gas (1930; left) in which the flickering, flame-like colours convey a message that is both direct and vibrant.

Hand-drawn lettering, consistently modern in style but rarely repeated, and vivid and energetic use of colour are the defining features of the work of French graphic designers of this period, who invented an advertising art of rare distinction while remaining true to the principles of fine art.

costumes and sets. Finally, Francis Bernard, a UAM member whose work is little known today, worked in a graphic style that was rigorous without being rigid, as seen in his posters for gas and the Arts Ménagers exhibition. His work for the publisher Paul Martial, with whom he regularly collaborated, made brilliant use of photography and photomontage: sadly the true extent of this exceptional body of work will never be known, as the firm's archives ended their life on a public refuse tip.

Press and publishing: advertising in all its forms

The development of graphic design in France is illustrated not only by poster art but also by the sumptuous brochures produced by the publishers Draeger (to whom Cassandre was under contract) and Tolmer, which celebrated luxury goods, cars and travel in unparalleled style. Equally opulent were the music-hall posters and programmes of Gesmar and Zig, and *Arts et Métiers Graphiques*, founded by Peignot and the most lavish magazine in its field. More opulence could be found in the *Gazette du Bon Ton* and the *Cahiers d'Art*. Only in *Vu*, launched by Lucien Vogel and with Alexander Liberman as its art director until his departure for New York, did modernism rear its head. And here again, between the brisk efficiency of the German *Gebrauchsgraphik* and the extreme artiness of *Arts et Métiers Graphiques*, the difference is almost palpable.

Another French magazine, *Vendre*, was founded by the Damour brothers, who also owned an ad agency and a studio that designed Art Deco posters. Early attempts at a scientific and commercial approach to advertising may be discerned the work of René-Louis Dupuy, and of Marcel Bleustein, founder

By 1937, advertising had unmistakably come of age. The UAM show devoted a large pavilion to it, in which the wine merchant Nicolas – who had commissioned advertising images from the greatest graphic designers, including Cassandre and Loupot (pioneer of photography and film in advertising) – proudly displayed its wares. Carlu produced an experimental 'luminograph' sign (below), an early attempt to create an open-air moving image, using programmed electric bulbs.

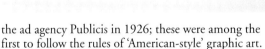

Paris, the capital of luxury, invented an advertising style to match. In 1927, shortly before he went bankrupt, the couturier Paul Poiret, a key figure, published an album entitled *Pan*, in which a page was devoted to each of the most prestigious brands. The design produced by the distinguished poster artist and illustrator Gus Bofa for couture house Madeleine Vionnet (left) was a model of elegance and restraint – qualities also to be found in all the brochures published by Draeger and Tolmer, as well as cover designs for the magazine *Arts et Métiers Graphiques* (above).

the ad agency Publicis in 1926; these were among the first to follow the rules of 'American-style' graphic art.

The 1937 exhibition, at which the still-persecuted UAM finally enjoyed a major presence, devoted an entire pavilion to advertising, under an electric luminograph by Carlu and with a massive mural by Cappiello: the *de facto* recognition of a real sea change.

Britain: insular design

Britain moved towards modernism in its own way. In typography, the Monotype Corporation under Stanley Morison and Beatrice Warde, both outstanding typographers with strong personalities, rejected the international style and opted instead to continue the heritage of the Arts and Crafts movement. Morison

•The luminograph was a system of electrically operated perforated strips, which made it possible to display whatever forms one wanted to the public in four colours.•

Jean Carlu

GILL SANS

Soaring to Success !

DAILY HERALD

— the Early Bird.

designed Times New Roman for *The Times* (and also redesigned the layout), but Monotype also commissioned Eric Gill's elegant sans serif typeface Gill Sans. Just as Cassandre dominated the field of graphic design in France, so Edward McKnight Kauffer came to dominate the British scene. Arriving in England from America, Kauffer revolutionized poster art in Britain with his 1919 poster for the *Daily Herald*. This was something completely new, both in its design and its layout. Though perhaps less powerful than Cassandre at his best, Kauffer was much more versatile: an accomplished illustrator and painter, he was equally at home with photomontage at its most sophisticated.

Kauffer's principal clients were the London Underground and Shell, and both of these companies became hugely influential in the development of graphic design in Britain. Frank Pick, who became publicity manager for London Transport just before the war, was

•The design *Flight* [left] was not invented in a studio. It came after much observation of birds in flight. The problem seemed...a translation into design terms of three factors... bird identification, movement, and formalization into pattern and line. Birds in flight and aeroplane formations are singularly alike. The arrowhead thrust is the dominant motif. But wings have a contrary movement – so this too has to be considered....•

E. McKnight
Kauffer, 1950

Above, Gill Sans typeface. Below, *The Times* before and after Morison's redesign.

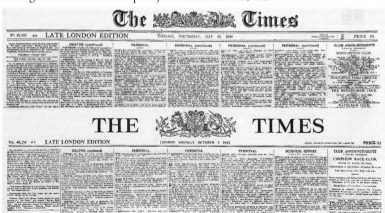

a towering figure who breathed life into every modernist domain with a rare sureness of touch. In 1916, he commissioned Edward Johnston to design a corporate sans serif typeface, Railway (later renamed Johnston), a model of its kind that became the first to be used on such a large scale. Later, in 1931, the famous stylized London Underground map appeared, becoming an icon of graphic

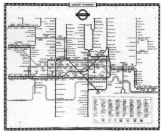

design, alongside the Underground logo by Zero (the pseudonym of Hans Schleger) and the refurbishment of tube stations by Eric Holden and Harold Stabler. Over the years, Pick commissioned hundreds of posters, not only from the cream of British graphic designers and painters but also from distinguished foreign talents such as Man Ray and László Moholy-Nagy. London Transport became not merely a means of getting around, but also a trusted companion to Londoners.

Meanwhile, Shell, under its director of publicity Jack Beddington, embarked on an equally ambitious and original project. It set out to change its image, camouflaging its status as a source of industrial pollution behind a campaign that encouraged the British to explore their countryside and historic monuments, with posters in pubs and on lorries bearing slogans such as 'To Visit British Landmarks'. In its 'These Men Use Shell' campaign, the company used gentle humour to suggest that many professions relied on its petrol.

Commissioned in 1933 from Henry C. Beck, the London Underground map (top), with the lines plotted vertically, horizontally or at forty-five degrees, was adopted as a model throughout the world. Although the real distance between stations varies, Beck chose to make them equidistant on the map in order to unify and clarify the network for passengers. The stations themselves also featured modernist graphics, such as Kauffer's huge photomontage at Earls Court (above).

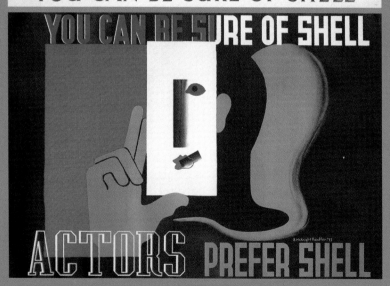

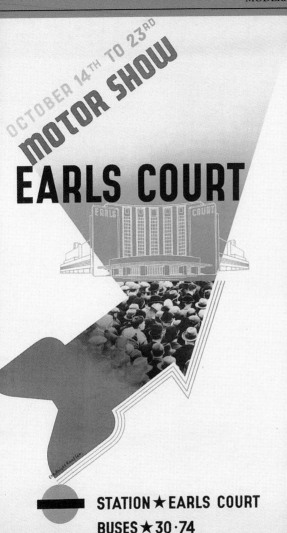

OCTOBER 14TH TO 23RD

MOTOR SHOW

EARLS COURT

EARLS COURT

STATION ★ EARLS COURT
BUSES ★ 30·74

London Transport and Shell were by far the biggest advertisers in Britain, due to two remarkable individuals. Frank Pick – described by Nikolaus Pevsner in the *Architectural Review* as 'the greatest patron of the arts whom this century has so far produced in England, and indeed the ideal patron for our age' – and Jack Beddington, publicity director of Shell from 1932. Both of them successfully reconciled art and advertising, employing both young artists and passing émigrés, and becoming involved in all aspects of design and architecture. Images by McKnight Kauffer (left and opposite below) were ubiquitous, while Hans Schleger, a German emigrant who worked under the name Zero, was given the chance to work as soon as he arrived, thanks to the openmindedness that characterized British advertising between the wars. His unusual poster for Shell (opposite above) was directly inspired by Surrealist painting.

Both of these firms gave commissions to Kauffer, who was equally at home with landscape painting as with photomontage, as is clear from his large-scale photomontage for Earl's Court Underground station and his montages for Aero. Other prominent names in design were also invited to contribute, including Austin Cooper, later principal of the Reimann School, and Tom Purvis, followed by Zero, Tom Eckersley, Eric Lombers and Tom Gentleman. One uniquely British aspect of these campaigns lay in the commissions awarded to fine artists of distinction, such as Graham Sutherland, Paul Nash, Barnett Freedman and Clifford and Rosemary Ellis, creating a distinctively British style.

Railway companies were other important clients: the London, Midland and Southern Railway, which adopted Gill Sans as its typeface, gave commissions to Cassandre and Alexander Alexeieff; the London and North Eastern Railway also chose Gill Sans, and commissioned a series of posters from Tom Purvis; these used flat colours to brilliantly rework the Beggarstaffs' style.

Meanwhile, two ad agencies explored the creative potential of the medium: S. H. Benson's, and especially Crawford's, who appointed one of the first great art directors, Ashley Havinden. His campaigns for Chrysler and Eno's Fruit Salts proved that high-quality graphic design and commercial advertising could be successfully combined.

Tom Purvis and his large poster in flat colours (below), Ashley Havinden's horsemen for Eno's Fruit Salts (opposite centre) and the silhouettes of Eckersley and Lombers's Post Office Film Display (opposite, above left) exemplify the best of the British Art Deco style, showing an obvious love of draughtsmanship and hand-drawn lettering.

F. C. Herrick and Shep were equally accomplished in their work for the Baynard Press, the largest printer in England.

With the arrival in the late 1930s of refugees fleeing the Nazi regime, insular Britain opened up to the influence of European avant-garde movements and Surrealism.

Art Deco in Europe

Throughout Europe, graphic design developed along similar lines, in the hands of a generation of designers who still favoured drawing over photography, working in a geometric and stylized manner; who did not adopt wholesale the principles of the new typography, but did choose sans serif faces; and who, most importantly, dispensed with the anecdotal approach in order to create posters that were clear, legible and effective, with text and images working together. In Munich, Ludwig Hohlwein and the Group of Six were the outstanding examples of this approach, which was also followed elsewhere in Germany by artists such as Wiertz and Engelhard. Austria had Joseph Binder (until he emigrated to America), Hungary had Bereny and Bortnyik, Czechoslovakia had Rotter and Zelenka, and Poland had Bartlomiejczyk and Tadeusz Gronowski,

Frantisek Zelenka's work clearly shows the variety of influences that co-existed in central Europe: when he used photography, as in a poster for Aero cars (above), he followed the example of Cassandre, resulting in a lightness and freedom of style.

⁕To reproduce the techniques of painting in a poster is to falsify it. But today, posters use new techniques. The first is photography, as distinct from illustration. …Typography is the second main theme in the modern poster. This means the most effective arrangement of lettering, and the choice of the right sizes and proportions…. The third main theme is colour…. This is the beating pulse, the consciousness and the vital principle of all posters.⁕

Frantisek Zelenka

a disciple of Cassandre. In Belgium, Leo Marfurt ranked among the best in his field; in Italy, Marcello Dudovich was joined by Federico Seneca, Marcello Nizzoli and Sepo (who also worked in France); and Spain had Josep Renau and Josep Morell.

Taken together, the work of all these artists – whether posters, brochures or advertisements – fits the style known today as Art Deco. With a few rare exceptions, this evolution in style did not alter the commissioning process, which still remained very much as in the world of fine art, with clients approaching graphic designers with commissions for posters. Working directly with their clients, graphic designers were spared the creative frustration of working for commercial agencies that would come later. The most prominent artists had agents: Maurice Moyrand of Alliance Graphique, for instance, found work for both Cassandre and Loupot.

Switzerland: the International Typographic Style

The rise of Nazism and Fascism forced large numbers of Europe's intellectual and artistic elite to flee their own countries. Italy was a special case: Leo Lionni left for New York, but Xanti Schawinsky returned again, and the young Max Huber arrived from Switzerland (although he returned there after war broke out). With the creation of Studio Boggeri in 1933 and clients such as Olivetti and Motta, Italy was primed to play a major part in the development of graphic design. The greatest beneficiaries of the pre-war artistic diaspora were Switzerland, which remained neutral, and of course the United States.

Switzerland had had a great tradition of art posters since 1908, when Emil Cardinaux's 'Zermatt' tourist poster appeared, and boasted a wealth of *affichistes*, as well as skilled printers. Dominating the field were the towering figures of Otto Baumberger in Zurich and Niklaus Stoecklin in Basel. In his work for the Baumann hat shop and the outfitter PKZ, Baumberger invented a new form of objectivity: the German *Sachplakat* that had

Here is one of the most powerful photomontages ever created, with a teeming crowd forming the body of Mussolini, text and images contained in the giant 'SI' ('Yes'), and an arrestingly coarse screen over the face. This genuinely avant-garde image is the work of Xanti Schawinsky, a Bauhaus-trained graphic designer who fled Fascism for a new life in America in 1936, at the invitation of Josef Albers – a happy accident for graphic design.

Featuring a hyper-realist overcoat with only the PKZ label to indicate that it is an advertisement, this poster by Otto Baumberger (left), dubbed the spiritual father of Swiss poster art, is a design landmark. The quality of the draughtsmanship and the audacity of the design – perhaps inspired by the painter Domenico Gnoli – remain as fresh today as when Baumberger created them.

Like Baumberger, Niklaus Stoecklin, leading artist of the Basel school, was able to switch styles with an

previously been flat now became three-dimensional. Stoecklin followed suit with his work for Binaca toothpaste, which looked forward to hyperrealism. As early as 1922, he designed a poster for the exhibition 'Der Buchdruck' (Book Printing) using typography alone – and Baumberger responded with his poster for Brak liqueur. Both artists were equally capable of symbolist minimalism or highly pictorial art (as in Stoecklin's work for Gaba throat lozenges or Baumberger's for PKZ), and both could turn their skills to any style or medium.

almost disconcerting ease. Who would guess that the Binaca toothpaste ad (page 59) and this poster for a printing exhibition (above) were by the same hand? In this respect, Swiss graphic design was certainly a cultural phenomenon like no other.

Herbert Matter trained under Cassandre and retained close links with him. His use of space was, like his mentor's, bold to the point of being truly revolutionary. In his series of posters for Swiss tourism, working from photographs that he had manipulated to accentuate contrasts (particularly the strong blue of the sky), he played with perspective effects or close-ups. This powerful image (left) is comparable with Cassandre's poster for the Davis Cup, in which a tennis ball in the foreground seems to be about to hit the viewer in the face – with the same startling impact as the glove has here.

•Lightning fast is my preferred shutter speed.... I follow the progress of colour photography with studious attention, and I am fascinated by home movies. Used in advertising, it always seems to me to lack colour. It is largely for this reason that I am going to try my luck in America. I hope that over there some cigarette or automobile company will place more lavish means at my disposal. Advertising in Europe is often not bold enough.•
Herbert Matter, *Arts et Métiers Graphiques*, no. 51, February 1936

Working alongside them were other talented artists; a series of posters commissioned by PKZ became a veritable showcase of contemporary artistic talent.

Ernst Keller taught in Zurich from 1918, training a generation of artists, including Walter Käch, Hermann Eidenbenz and Theo Ballner, in photography and the new typography. Anton Stankowski, formerly assistant to Max Burchartz in Germany, worked in Zurich from 1929 to 1937, using a style that combined photography with the Akzidenz Grotesk typeface. His poster for Liebig stock cubes, designed with Hans Neuburg in 1934, is a model of its kind. Max Bill also arrived from Germany, gathering around him the Swiss Constructivists (Lohse, Neuburg, Vivarelli and Huber). Finally, in 1933, Jan Tschichold also chose exile in Switzerland.

These artists and their teaching were to become major influences, giving rise after the war to the International Typographic Style that Switzerland would export throughout the world. This was a rationalist and visually highly disciplined style, using modular typographical grids with the addition of photography where necessary. With the masterly series of posters he designed between 1934 and 1936, Herbert Matter brought about a revolution in both photography and travel posters. Their dynamic use of space and violent colour contrasts brought these iconic images such success that Matter decided to set off to conquer New York.

America, land of promise

America had always been the favoured destination for emigrants from Europe. Lucian Bernhard in 1923, M. F. Agha in 1928 and Alexey Brodovitch in 1930 all moved to America to further their careers. Following Hitler's rise to power, a large number of Europe's artistic, intellectual and scientific elites went into exile for political reasons. Josef Albers and Joseph Binder were among those who arrived in 1933, to be followed by Walter Gropius, László Moholy-Nagy (founders of the New Bauhaus in Chicago), Herbert Bayer and Will Burtin in 1937, Ladislav Sutnar in 1939 and Alexander Liberman in 1940. This haemorrhage was a cultural windfall for the United States, which until the early 1930s had lagged behind Europe in levels of artistic innovation.

Although major advertising agencies were now being set up, such as Lord & Thomas founded by Albert Lasker, the father of modern publicity, campaigns were

In another Swiss paradox, the strict theoretician and teacher Ernst Keller displayed a heady freedom in his own work. For an exhibition on tobacco (above), he used a daringly 'primitive' image that overlaps with the bold typography with half of the capital 'T' cut off – a good demonstration of the truth that, for those who have truly mastered them, rules are made to be broken.

An ad for Palmolive soap (top) embodies the old-fashioned advertising style still prevalent in the US until the 1930s.

The magical, twirling Hartmans

Agha pioneered a whole new look for fashion magazines. Having worked in Berlin, he knew all the young talents in Europe, and commissioned them to design covers for him (below). But it was in his approach to design and photography that he was most innovative. He was the first to use cut-out photographs and to lay out images in a way that echoed the subject matter of the article in visual form. His 'Dance' layout from *Vanity Fair*, 1936 (left), with its overlapping photographs arranged in order of size, remains an archetype of its kind.

still built around slogans, such as Palmolive's 'Keep that schoolgirl complexion', accompanied by illustrations that were often flat and banal. The press, later to be the agent of change, would risk nothing more outré than Erté, who designed cover art for *Harper's Bazaar*. New York had boasted an Art Directors' Club since 1920: now the only thing it lacked was genuine art directors.

The advent of the art director

In 1928, Condé Nast, editor of *Vogue* and *Vanity Fair*, brought M. F. Agha to America from Berlin. Born in Kiev to Turkish parents, the autocratic and overbearing Dr Agha, as he liked to style himself, revolutionized magazine design. Adopting sans serif faces for the text, he commissioned images from the best contemporary photographers, such as Steichen, Horst, Weston and Abbott, and from the finest European artists for *Vanity Fair*. The first art director to work in double-page spreads, he also introduced colour photographs and cut-out images. His department quickly became a hotbed of new talent.

In 1934, *Harper's Bazaar* brought Alexey Brodovitch over from Paris, where he was at the height of his success. An award-winner at the 1925 Paris exhibition and subsequently appointed art director to the Trois Quartiers store chain and the magazine *Arts et Métiers Graphiques*, he nevertheless chose to go and teach in Philadelphia – where he worked for the rest of his life,

•Brodovitch's use of film as a model for the graphic appearance of *Harper's Bazaar* extended to the entire editorial "well", or center section of the magazine. With Carmel Snow's collaboration, he sequenced each issue's pages to provide the most dramatic visual progression possible. While he almost always balanced his experimental pages with quiet, relatively conventional spreads, he made the act of perusing an issue visually compelling. No previous publication designer had understood so thoroughly the linkage of graphic display and temporal experience.•

Andy Grundberg
on Alexey Brodovitch
(left, photographed by
Richard Avedon)

in his own studios. An inspired teacher and art director, he brought in Cassandre, André Derain, Marcel Vertes, Saul Steinberg and others to design covers, and trained Irving Penn and Richard Avedon. Conceived as a series of double-page spreads that flowed smoothly from one article to the next, the magazine became a testing ground for new ideas. Where it led, the rest of the field followed. In 1938, *Fortune*, the most expensive and opulent of them all, replaced the ultra-traditionalist and anti-modernist Thomas Cleland with John Brennan, who in turn commissioned Matter, Sutnar, Bayer and Cassandre.

Advertising was also changing, as posters gradually cast off the shackles of realism. Much of the credit for this

Opposite below, *Vanity Fair* covers by Raoul Dufy (August 1934, above) and Paolo Garretto (June 1934, below). Top, *Harper's Bazaar* cover by A. M. Cassandre.

must go to Otis Shepard, art director for the poster designers Forster Kleiser from 1927, who from 1932 (for thirty years, as it turned out) designed campaigns for Wrigley's in the spirit of European Art Deco. Sascha Maurer, who arrived in 1925, produced posters for the Pennsylvanian Railway and other tourist sites that raised

American poster art to the levels of the best to be found in Europe. But the first modernist graphic designer to cast off European influences and find a wholly American idiom was American-born Lester Beall. His style was clear, direct, functional and informative, and in 1937 he produced a series of posters for the Rural Electrification Administration that were models of simplicity.

Ad agencies were also changing. Earnest Elmo Calkins, of Calkins & Holden, had been first to use illustrators such as Montgomery Flagg and Leyendecker, and later commissioned work from Cubist and Futurist painters.

Just before the Second World War, a new generation of artists – including Sascha Maurer (poster, above right) and Cassandre (below, poster for Ford, his only large-scale work in the US) – redefined American graphic design. Above left, logo for the NRA by Charles Coiner.

He also pioneered the use of a 'creative team' of art director and copywriter, working in tandem. At Ayer and Co. in Philadelphia, always the most forward-thinking of the big agencies, Charles Coiner was the first to hire Maurer, Shepard, Klinger, Kauffer and Binder, then later, as the waves of immigrants increased, Bayer, Carlu, Matter, Léger and Kepes. The story goes that when Cassandre disembarked in New York, Coiner was waiting for him on the waterfront with a contract in his pocket, ready to be signed. For a campaign for Doyle pineapples he turned to Noguchi, O'Keeffe and Cassandre, and for De Beers diamonds to Dufy, Picasso, Derain and Covarrubias. His entire working life was 'a battle against ugliness', but his finest hour came with his collaboration with Walter Paepcke, head of the CCA (Container Corporation of America), manufacturers of cardboard boxes and packaging. Starting from the principle that he was seeking to sell an image of society rather than of cardboard boxes, he and Paepcke together created the first ever corporate identity for an American firm. From 1936, the 'house style' was established, with posters by Cassandre, to be followed after America joined the war by the 'Paperboard Goes to War' campaign, with images by Bayer, Carlu, Matter and Leo Lionni.

By 1940, a new generation of designers trained by Europe's finest was ready to challenge the creative supremacy of their European colleagues. William Golden, Alvin Lustig, Bradbury Thompson, Paul Rand and Saul Bass, to name only a few, were ready to set out, with a victorious America, to conquer the world.

Lester Beall was the first US designer to create images were truly free of European influences. His poster series for the Rural Electrification Administration, made up of simple ideograms stripped of all geometric superfluities, and with unashamedly plain typography, may be considered the earliest example of true American graphic design, modern and free. More direct and more purist than Art Deco, this poster heralds the graphic design of the post-war period.

Westvaco
Inspirations from contemporary advertising art
for Printers

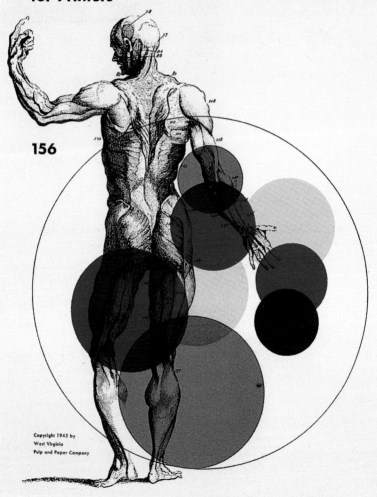

156

In the aftermath of the Second World War, the American advertising industry began to absorb both artists and innovative ideas imported from Europe. The art director was king and the 'big idea' the ruling concept. Meanwhile, the Basel School in Switzerland continued the pioneering work of the Bauhaus, exporting the International Typographic Style to the rest of the world.

CHAPTER 4

INTERNATIONAL INNOVATIONS

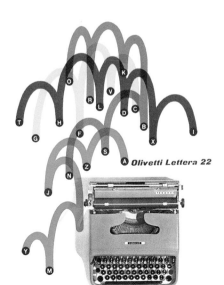

Triumphant and free, advertising now dared to use bright colours, as in these two examples (opposite, publicity brochure by the American Bradbury Thompson for the paper manufacturer Westvaco, 1953; right, Italian poster for Olivetti by Giovanni Pintori, *c.* 1953). The layout remains impeccable, but the stiffness of the pre-war period has vanished.

Olivetti Lettera 22

Think small.

Our little car isn't so much of a novelty
any more.
 A couple of dozen college kids don't
try to squeeze inside it.
 The guy at the gas station doesn't ask
where the gas goes.
 Nobody even stares at our shape.
 In fact, some people who drive our little
flivver don't even think 32 miles to the gal-
lon is going any great guns.
 Or using five pints of oil instead of five
quarts.
 Or never needing anti-freeze.
 Or racking up 40,000 miles on a set of
tires.
 That's because once you get used to
some of our economies, you don't even
think about them any more.
 Except when you squeeze into a small
parking spot. Or renew your small insur-
ance. Or pay a small repair bill.
 Or trade in your old VW for a
new one.
 Think it over.

The Volkswagen account (left) was made for Bill Bernbach. At a time when big US-made cars were in their chrome-trimmed heyday, this small and (relevant in the sensitive post-war period) German-made car clearly required a sales pitch that was radical and new. Helmut Krone, art director (and disciple of Brodovitch), laid down guidelines at the outset that held

good throughout the campaign. The image occupied two-thirds of the available space, usually in the form of a small photo on a white background. The impact of this unlikely and invariably provocative combination of elements was then supported by an explanatory text: the earliest slogan, 'Think small', became an advertising classic. DDB caught its rivals off-guard and the rest is history. In 1963, Avis – the second largest car hire firm in America – followed suit with a campaign under the slogan 'We try harder'.

Europeans head the field in America

The cream of European graphic designers had emigrated to America, where they made a major contribution to the war effort, and in so doing, demonstrated the effectiveness of their approach to graphic design. Examples of this range from posters by Carlu, Lionni and Matter and exhibitions organized by Bayer to practical manuals for the air force by Burtin.

 After victory had been secured, the economy boomed in a world now governed by business and industry. Magazine publishing had been the pioneer industry in opening the way to modernism, but now it was now joined by the great American corporations, later to become the multinationals – and everything changed.

America had already invented the ad agency, the sole mechanism capable of responding to the needs of advertisers. Within a few years a new advertising industry had emerged, based on Madison Avenue. Two of its most legendary figures, copywriter Bill Bernbach and art director Paul Rand, both Americans familiar with European culture, had first met in the Weintraub agency in the early 1940s. Both rejected the scientific approach to advertising: their credo was based on the power of art. Their approach became known as the 'big idea'. It was ad campaigns that would now forge a brand's future, using sheer creativity to surprise a startled public and turn preconceived notions on their heads. As Paul Rand observed, the spectator's role in this process was an active one, for he or she was expected to complete the message.

Bernbach, who set up the DDB agency in 1949, started out with modest clients such as Levy's bread or Orbach, although many of thse grew into giants, including Polaroid and most famously Volkswagen, who commissioned his best-known campaign. The agency became a hotbed of new talent, with designers such as Gene Federico, who created an historic campaign for *Woman's Day* and eventually founded his own agency, and George Lois, who took over *Esquire* before also founding his own agency. Paul Rand, meanwhile, was creative director of the Weintraub agency from 1941 to 1954 before setting up on his own. His great contribution came in response to another pressing demand from the large corporations: the need to build a corporate identity. For IBM, for example, Rand designed not only a logo but also the IBM Design Guide, the

A logo, and by extension a visual house style, was now a prerequisite for any business. The most prolific and original of the many graphic designers working in this field was Paul Rand. Whether it was a playful puzzle-like image for Westinghouse (opposite right), or the diminutive parcel topping the UPS of United Parcel Service, or the circle within a circle of the ABC television network, Rand's solutions were always witty, based on a premise that was playful, immediate and made sense. In 1981 he convinced his client IBM to use a rebus that offered a beguiling twist on the computer giant's corporate image (below).

Left, Charles Coiner, coordinator of the American public information service during the Second World War, holding a copy of Jean Carlu's 1941 poster, *America's Answer: Production.*

first attempt on this scale to impose a visual house style on every aspect of the business. He later did the same for Westinghouse.

In the 1950s, advertising was at the heart of a explosion of creativity, in which both European designers and their American counterparts – all having absorbed influences ranging from Bauhaus to Surrealism – found fertile ground for their imaginations. For Knoll, Herbert Matter first reduced the company trademark or logo to a simple 'K', before devising

From illustration to stylization (opposite centre, poster by Tomi Ungerer for the *New*

She's got to **go out** to get Woman's Day

revolutionary campaigns in which the image alone carried the message. Ladislav Sutner was art director for Sweet's retail catalogues for twenty years, designing complex layouts, and in 1941 publishing *Catalog Design Progress*. In 1948, Will Burtin took over from Lester Beall as art director of *Scope*, the house magazine of Upjohn pharmaceutical labs, where he made science accessible and comprehensible to a lay audience, through techniques such as his ground-breaking use of hugely enlarged three-dimensional models of a single blood cell and of the human brain. Erik Nitsche, later to

York Times) and photography (above, ad for *Woman's Day* by Gene Federico, 1953), art directors constantly sought new images to catch the public's attention and put the message across.

Top, William Golden's logo for CBS, 1951.

revolutionize the visual house style of General Dynamics, successfully tackled the abstract notion of 'Atoms for Peace' for a series of posters in 1955. Walter H. Allner, who arrived in the US in 1949, became design consultant to RCA and Johnson & Johnson. Henry Wolf moved from *Esquire* to *Harper's Bazaar*, where he took over from Brodovitch. And from his position as art director of *Vogue*, Alexander Liberman extended his influence to the whole of the Condé Nast group.

The 'new advertising' in America

Over a period of more than twenty years, William Golden, aided by Lou Dorfsman, developed a corporate image for CBS, starting with an eye logo. Bradbury Thompson produced his 'Inspirations' for the paper manufacturer Westvaco. Working on interior decoration magazines in New York and Los Angeles, Alvin Lustig raised the art of avant-garde page layout to virtuoso heights. Lou Silverstein redesigned the *New York Times*, and Herb Lubalin did the same for the *Saturday Evening Post*, introducing radical changes that – though shocking at the time – helped the public to adapt to a new era in typography. Saul Bass worked for ABC and became best known for his work with the film director and producer Otto Preminger, transforming film posters, titles and graphics with his designs for *The Man with the Golden Arm* and *Exodus*. American advertising displayed a wealth of exuberance and variety that was genuinely impressive. As well as calling on the world's best typographers and photographers, it also channelled the talents of its best cartoonists and illustrators, including Ronald Searle, Bob Blechmann, Ben Shahn and the cream of French talent of the period: Tomi Ungerer in New York, André François and Raymond Savignac.

American advertising in its Golden Age was notable for its huge variety, with no single dominant trend as there had been before the war. Creativity was the new watchword, leading to cutting-edge design – such as Saul Bass's movie posters and title sequences (bottom) – and innovative photography and typography. The heirs of Brodovitch were in their element.

In the early 1960s, there was quite simply an explosion in the publicity market. Graphic design was now no longer a single profession, but had fragmented into a number of different functions, each requiring different skills. The design concept was now key. While the success of a major advertising campaign might not necessarily be in direct proportion to the calibre of its graphic design, stylish presentation of company logos, corporate images and annual reports was vital to imply a general level of excellence. Among the booming number of design studios was Chermayeff & Geismar Associates in New York, who specialized in exhibition work (the American pavilion at the 1958 Brussels World Fair was their first major

site) and also designed corporate images for many large corporations and institutions such as Mobil, Xerox and MoMA. Another major agency was Unimark in Chicago, founded by Massimo Vignelli and Bob Noorda.

Swiss graphic design

This rational and objective approach opened the door for the Basel School and Swiss graphic design in general, whose influence was spread worldwide by the design magazine *Graphis*, edited by Walter Herdeg. The cornerstone of Swiss graphics was Emil Ruder, a tireless teacher in Basel from 1947 to 1970. In the vanguard of the movement – in which space was strictly organized according to typographical grids – was Karl Gerstner. Having worked for Geigi laboratories, Gerstner set up the GGK agency in order to put his principles into practice, and quickly scooped major contracts such as Volkswagen's Swiss account. The magazine *Neue Grafik* was launched in 1958 by Josef Müller-Brockmann, Hans Neuburg, Carlo Vivarelli and Richard P. Lohse, all, with Armin Hofmann, dedicated to the stringently austere *Konstruktive Graphik*. Sans serif typefaces were de rigueur: Adrian Frutiger designed Univers, while Max Miedinger and Edouard Hoffman produced Helvetica.

The Swiss were the undisputed masters of typography. Words and images were combined according to these strict principles, and almost exclusively in black and white. Müller-Brockmann's series of road safety posters,

American exuberance found its match in Swiss stringency. The typefaces Helvetica (opposite, below) and Univers, combined with photography, were the tools of the new Constructivism, technically and formally perfect but cold (opposite, poster by Vivarelli, and below, by Müller-Brockmann). However, the style grew popular in America, where its crisp gravitas appealed to corporations for use on stationery and annual reports (left, Mobil logo and opposite centre, typographic grid by Emil Ruder, 1967).

Vivarelli's 'Für das Alter' (the first use of vertical lettering) and Armin Hofmann's *Giselle* are all masterpieces of composition and power. In his 'Musica Viva' poster series, Müller-Brockmann echoed musical composition by designing typographical grids with infinite variations. A similarly demanding approach is found in the early work of Siegfried Odermatt and Rosmarie Tissi. Their writings and their teachings – both within Switzerland, which attracted students from across the world, and abroad (Hofmann taught at Yale, for instance) – meant that

Swiss graphic designers left no corner of the
world untouched by their influence.

Germany, Italy and the Netherlands

Switzerland was not alone in carrying the
torch for Bauhaus design: at the Institute of
Design in Ulm, Germany, Otl Aicher and
the prolific Max Bill also sought to revive it.
Between 1951 and 1968 the school, which
pioneered a semiological approach to
advertising, was renowned chiefly for its work
in the field of industrial design. Aicher also
put his own rigorous approach into practice
in his corporate design for Lufthansa and his
design system for the Munich Olympics. In
Kassel – home of the Dokumenta exhibitions,
the third of which in 1964 was devoted to
design – teachers such as Karl Oskar Blase and Arnold
Bode trained students including Gunter Rambow and
Hans Hillmann, who in turn taught Friede Grindler.

In Stuttgart, Anton Stankowski was following a similar
path. Hans Michel and Gunter Kieser designed record
sleeves and posters, and in 1959 Willy Fleckhaus
launched the magazine *Twen*. Along with *Elle*, launched
in France in the same year, it became a key magazine of
the period. This was also the year in which Michael
Engelmann, who had returned from America in 1949,
began his outstanding advertising campaigns for Roth-
Händle cigarettes and Bols liqueurs, later to be taken
over by Mandel & Oberer. German foundries remained
at the forefront of typography: in 1958, Hermann Zapf
designed the typeface Optima.

In Italy, meanwhile, several designers returned from
exile after the war, including Max Huber who, with Luigi
Veronesi and Remo Muratore, founded the Rinascita
school of advertising in Milan. Erberto Carboni and
the Studio Boggeri, with which Max Huber was
closely associated, largely completed the Milan school.
Here, unlike in Switzerland, constructivism was not
synonymous with rigidity. For the department store La
Rinascente, Max Huber combined ancient and modern,
using Bodoni Italic for the definite article and Futura

American designers
proved that
photography and
typography need know
no bounds. Michael
Engelmann, who had
spent many years in the
US, offered another
demonstration of this in
his work in Germany for
Roth-Händle cigarettes
(below), in which he
juxtaposed a cigarette
and a hand – always in
red, like the brand's
trademark red packet.

Max Huber, a Swiss designer working in Italy, also adopted an exuberant, sensual approach, casting off the strictures of Constructivism in no uncertain fashion. In this poster (left), his love of jazz erupted into a composition in which circles of varying sizes evoke the sound of the drums.

In this poster for an American exhibition in Zurich (opposite above), Max Bill made energetic use of his lively brand of Constructivism.

Bold for the name. For the Monza racing circuit, he created layers of typography and overlapping perspectives that invoked both freedom and rushing speed. With Giovanni Pintori as its art director between 1950 and 1968, and using work by Marcello Nizzoli, Raymond Savignac, Milton Glaser and Jean-Michel Folon, Olivetti advertised its wares in a distinctive style combining primary colours and a playful approach to design.

Pirelli commissioned work from the same names and also from Armando Testa, who opened his own agency. These designers – along with Franco Grignani's experimental photography, playing on sensual curves, for the photo-typesetter Alfieri & Lacroix and Bruno Munari's use of colourful collage for Campari – allowed Italy to escape the rigidity which in other countries robbed design of its originality.

In the Netherlands, home of De Stijl, Wim Crouwel remained faithful to the International Typographic Style and to functionalist principles. In 1963 he founded the group Total Design, which designed a comprehensive signage scheme for Amsterdam's Schiphol airport and soon expanded internationally. During the 1960s, Crouwel also designed new fonts for the computer age. Pieter Brattinga applied similar principles in his *Kwadraat-Bladen* (Quadrat prints). Another major figure was Willem Sandberg, art director of the Stedelijk Museum in Amsterdam; his experiments with simple, apparently improvised typography followed the style of Hendrik Werkman.

A bove, cover of the typographic catalogue *New Alphabet* (1967) by the Dutch designer Wim Crouwel.

France, a culture apart

With the work of Raymond Savignac and Bernard Villemot, France continued the tradition of *affichistes* who produced poster art: conceiving an idea and giving it free

graphic expression in their own individual style. Savignac came to prominence in 1949 when he created the Monsavon cow, and his humorous, cartoonlike images breathed new life into French advertising. Using a faux-naif drawing style and bright colours, he worked for many French brands, using ideas that were dazzlingly simple: a traffic jam running through a man's head for Aspro headache pills, or the front end of a bull savouring the scent of a stew made from its hindquarters for Maggi stock cubes. Savignac's campaigns for Bic, Frigéco and Air France were hugely influential; his work was soon in international demand and attracted followers such as Hervé Morvan in France, Herbert Leupin in Switzerland (previously a realist) and Julian Key in Belgium.

•If I express myself through jokes, conceits and caprices, if my posters are just visual clowning, this is primarily because people find their daily routines so profoundly dreary that I believe it is the duty of advertising to offer them a little fun.•

Raymond Savignac
(Maggi poster above)

Bernard Villemot's painterly posters were graphic adaptations of the painting of the Paris school. His campaigns for Bally and Orangina were classics of their time. André François meanwhile used pastel and soft lead pencil to create a poetic universe for Citroën and Printemps stores, while many of Jean-Michel Folon's memorable images contain a little man in a hat.

In the field of typography, away from the international mainstream and sheltered from the rigid canons of the new typography, French designers held their own. Marcel Jacno invented the Gauloises packet and the

Savignac and Villemot, who maintained their dominant position in billboard advertising into the 1970s, were old friends and colleagues. Both came to public attention in 1949 through an exhibition at which Savignac sold his Monsavon cow to L'Oréal. At this time the American system of advertising agencies had not yet arrived in France: agencies such as Etablissements de la Vasselais would visit clients to sell them visuals produced by *affichistes*. Savignac worked directly with major clients such as Bic, as did Villemot with Bally shoes (left). As a result, French posters retained the artistic flavour and a particular kind of humour and charm that lithography still possesses. Early attempts at using photography in French advertising were inconclusive and often dull, but the days of the freelance *affichiste* were nevertheless numbered.

France-Soir masthead. His work for the Théâtre National Populaire – where he took the stencilled lettering that touring theatre groups used on their prop boxes as his inspiration for his Chaillot typeface – was both witty and original. For the Olive foundry, Roger Excoffon designed highly successful typefaces for commercial use (in signs and catalogues), such as Choc and Mistral, as well as

In 1960, the arrival of photo-typesetting gave graphic designers a new freedom. Working with the photographer Henry Cohen, Massin made exemplary use of this opportunity. His edition

working for Air France. Specializing in the fields of fashion and theatre, René Gruau drew inimitably chic Parisian ladies. René Ferracci, meanwhile, dragged cinema advertising away from stodgy realism with his startling use of photomontage.

The world of book publishing also had its own specifically French flavour. From 1946, Pierre Faucheux experimented freely with juxtapositions of different styles and typefaces in editions for the Club Français du Livre. In 1962, one of his assistants, Robert Massin, reworked his ground-breaking edition of Raymond Queneau's *Exercices de Style*, following this in 1964 with an edition of Ionesco's *La Cantatrice Chauve (The Bald Soprano)* presented as a photo-story that made brilliant use of photographic manipulation of text and images. Working

of Ionesco's play *La Cantatrice Chauve* (*The Bald Soprano*; above) was an 'intelligent' photo-story, with each character given his or her own typeface, with the women all 'speaking' in italic. The type varied in size according to the tone of the conversation, and was intercut with blank pages of silence. Cieslewicz, meanwhile, revolutionized the use of photography with his manipulated images and photomontages (opposite, above).

for Gallimard from 1958, Massin left an indelible impression on the whole of French publishing.

An influx of Swiss and Polish talent

France also played host to a group of Swiss graphic designers who pulled French design into line with international trends: working for Peignot, Adrian Frutiger produced the typeface Univers; Albert Hollenstein worked in photo-typesetting; and – most influentially of all – Peter Knapp became art director of *Elle*, founded by Hélène Gordon-Lazareff on her return from the United States. Using sans serif typefaces, Knapp designed daring page layouts, and employed a new generation of photographers that included David Bailey, Guy Bourdin, Helmut Newton and Frank Horvat. Jean Widmer also came to France, taking over Knapp's old job as art director for Galeries Lafayette.

The Polish designer Jan Lenica arrived in Paris in 1963 and pursued his technique of making dramatic collages before moving into film animation. His compatriot Roman Cieslewicz, who arrived in the same year, was successively art director of *Vogue* and *Elle* (where he succeeded Knapp), then of *Mafia* and *Opus International*. Using the techniques of collage and photomontage, he sent shockwaves through the world of advertising with his work for clients including the fashion designer Charles Jourdan, before turning to work in the public sector.

Creativity in Britain

In Britain, the designers who had been catalysts

Although his name is almost forgotten, Marcel Jacno's work has been a part of French life for many years, since he designed the masthead of the newspaper *France-Soir* and redesigned the packaging for Gauloises cigarettes (below), representing sales of some two billion since the early 1980s.

Left and above, designs for the Univers typeface by Adrian Frutiger.

for change before the war – including F. H. K. Henrion and Hans Schleger (formerly known as Zero) – now opened their own design studios or advertising agencies, where they handled major accounts: Henrion secured KLM and British Leyland, for instance. Jan Tschichold moved to London, where he worked for Penguin Books, going against the prevailing trend by reintroducing serif typefaces. Ashley Havinden was still in charge of Crawford's. With the founding of the Design Research Unit, which specialized in designing corporate images for clients including British Rail and Dunlop, Britain was poised to become a major international player in the field. Further progress came with the arrival of American designers Bob Gill, who went into partnership with Alan Fletcher and Colin Forbes in a prefiguration of Pentagram, and Robert Brownjohn, former partner in Chermayeff & Geismar, who joined J. Walter Thompson and created the titles for *Goldfinger* in 1964. Minale, Tattersfield & Partners (founded in 1964) and Wolff-Olins (founded in 1965) were typical examples of agencies who specialized in working with the major clients who were gaining a foothold in London, paving the way for a new type of design service for the worlds of commerce and industry.

A new kind of advertising

The approach adopted by ad agencies became increasingly scientific, relying on tests and studies, on media plans and international strategies, with the result that the creative aspects of the profession, although remaining in theory the preserve of the creative team of art director and copywriter, in fact began

B ritain was quick to adopt the American style, following the example of leading poster designers such as F. H. K. Henrion (above, KLM logo, 1958) and Hans Schleger, who opened highly specialized design studios concentrating on corporate branding. The major American ad agencies lost no time in opening London offices, so propelling Britain to the cutting edge of European advertising in the 1980s (top, Alan Fletcher, poster for the 100th Year of the Automobile exhibition, 1986; left, British Rail logo, 1952; left below, Robert Brownjohn, record sleeve for Machito & His Orchestra, 1959).

Sheringham

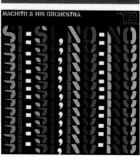

MACHITO & HIS ORCHESTRA

to pass through the hands of an ever-growing number of extra players.

In the process, the world of graphic design was increasingly left behind – although Britain in the 1980s still encouraged the occasional digression into Surrealist ingenuity, such as Collett Dickenson Pearce's campaigns for Benson & Hedges and Paul Arden's at Saatchi & Saatchi for Silk Cut. In Paris, Robert Delpire commissioned work for Citroën from André François, Roland Topor and William Klein; in Germany, Heinz Edelmann at Putz often worked with Tomi Ungerer; but these were the exceptions. More and more agencies were swallowed up by giant companies with offices on every continent and specialists in every area of publicity. The power to shock or surprise was now limited to a sprinkling of advertisers, most of them in the field of fashion: Nike, through Wieden & Kennedy, set out to

Robert Delpire is a champion of the equal partnership of art and advertising. From the art magazine *Neuf*, which he founded at the age of twenty-three, to *L'Oeil*, of which he was art director for eight years, he moved to the world of advertising (above, campaign for Citroën). He also publishes and exhibits works by designers and photographers such as Henri Cartier-Bresson, Robert Doisneau and Brassaï, and illustrators such as André François.

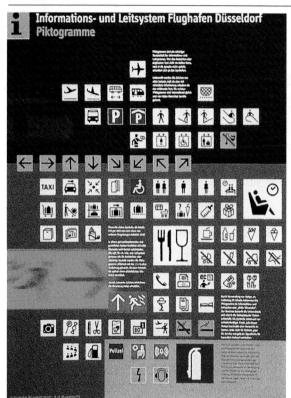

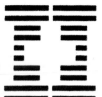

As public transport systems grew, so there became a need for an international language of signs for travellers. Otto and Maria Neurath were pioneers in this field with their Isotype system. In 1965, Total Design in Amsterdam created the first clear and unified signing system for Schiphol airport, which became a model for others. The group subsequently created a similar system for Düsseldorf airport, recently revised by MetaDesign (left). Pictograms soon became ubiquitous. Vignelli and Noorda redesigned the signage for the New York subway, and Jean Widmer did the same for French motorways. Hospitals (above), museums, stations – the big design groups now competed for a massive market. Updating the graphics of major institutions was also a huge field, such as Studio Dumbar's work for the Dutch post office (brochure, opposite centre).

appeal to the youth market, while Benetton, working directly with Oliviero Toscani and without an agency, caused a sensation with its posters and with its magazine, *Colors*, designed by Tibor Kalman.

Industry, too, required logos, house styles and packaging designs. Raymond Loewy, famous for his redesign of Lucky Strike cigarettes and the leader in the field, managed to maintain a presence in New York (where he was based), London and Paris simultaneously. Following the example of Pentagram, founded in London by Colin Forbes and Alan Fletcher and soon established internationally, graphic designers formed studios or groups. Wim Crouwel's Total Design in the Netherlands was soon joined by Studio Dumbar (with

It was a meeting in 1983 between Oliviero Toscani and Luciano Benetton that gave rise to the most controversial advertising campaign of the late 20th century (left, Benetton poster in the Paris Métro). Cutting out the use of an agency – this alone was enough to raise the hackles of the advertising world – and working mainly through posters carrying

whom they worked in partnership for the Dutch post office) and Olaf Leu Design in Frankfurt. Erik Spiekermann, trained by Henrion in London, founded MetaDesign in Berlin, while in France, groups such as Carré Noir appeared. In New York this field flourished, and the

Swiss system offered the perfect answer for businesses in search of impeccably presented annual reports to maintain the confidence of their shareholders: Vignelli & Associates and their disciple Rudolf de Harak were the embodiment of this crisp typography, and Chermayeff & Geismar called on the services of Swiss artist Stefan Geissbühler.

But the time for critical self-appraisal was now approaching. Wolfgang Weingart, a teacher at the Basel School, challenged the entire system and freed typography from any remaining constraints. Young American designers such as April Greiman and Dan Friedman trained with him, and Katherine McCoy disseminated his ideas at the prestigious Cranbrook Academy of Art in Detroit. Robert Venturi, who in 1965 wrote *Complexity and Contradiction in Architecture*, was also extremely influential, inspiring postmodernism and offering a serious alternative style for new advertisers to co-opt if they chose.

only the slogan 'United Colors of Benetton', they appropriated the world's social problems in order to put across their message, without referring to Benetton products themselves.

•So what are we gonna do? What can individuals do to ensure that this planet doesn't self-destruct? I can only come up with one solution: everyone get involved. And that's where the imagery involved in the Benetton ads stands head and shoulders above the rest.•
Spike Lee,
Rolling Stone, 1992

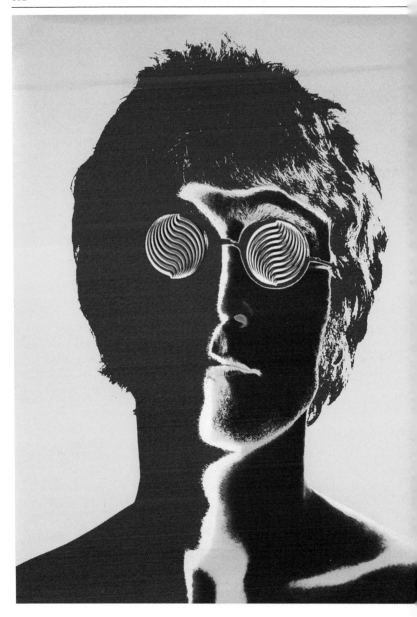

Committed to their ideals and unwilling to become involved in advertising, a generation of graphic designers made a place for themselves in the public sphere, making images inspired by contemporary social and political issues. In the 1980s and 1990s, the arrival of computers, along with the imagery of rock music and virtual reality, precipitated another revolution in graphic design.

CHAPTER 5

FROM POLITICAL ACTIVISM TO THE DIGITAL AGE

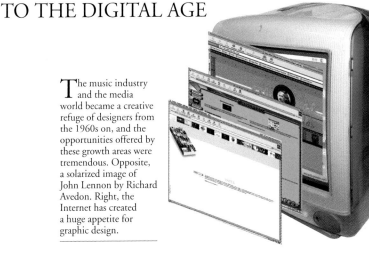

The music industry and the media world became a creative refuge of designers from the 1960s on, and the opportunities offered by these growth areas were tremendous. Opposite, a solarized image of John Lennon by Richard Avedon. Right, the Internet has created a huge appetite for graphic design.

Protest and revolution

Although the International Typographic Style had triumphed, its victory was now under threat. The impersonal Swiss system all too easily drained design of its originality, and – more importantly – the children of the post-war baby-boom generation no longer viewed the values of Western society with unquestioning acceptance. The year 1967 was a milestone in many ways: it was the year in which Andy Warhol designed his banana album cover for the Velvet Underground; Peter Blake created the Beatles' *Sergeant Pepper's Lonely Hearts Club Band*; Milton Glaser produced his Bob Dylan poster; and Robert Crumb designed his legendary cover for Big Brother and the Holding Company. Pop music was now a major force and the catalyst for innovations to come. *Rolling Stone* was born, as was *Fact*, founded by Ralph Ginzburg with Herb Lubalin as its art director.

This movement had been foreshadowed by the Push Pin Studio in New York, founded in 1954 by Milton Glaser, Seymour Chwast and others. Using Renaissance typefaces and Victorian and Art Nouveau influences, it provided alternatives to the International Typographic Style. In 1964, Art Kunkin launched the *L. A. Free Press*, the first underground newspaper. Two years later, Victor Moscoso founded *Neon Rose*, and the first posters for pop concerts at the Fillmore Auditorium and Avalon Ballroom appeared in San Francisco, signed by designers such as Mouse, Kelley, Wilson and Griffin. Psychedelic posters, heavily influenced by LSD and cannabis, created

First published in 1964 as the cover of the satirical magazine *Monocle*, 'Black Power, White Power' by Tomi Ungerer was published in poster form by Rhinoceros Press, co-founded by Ungerer himself. He bombarded America with his images of protest and, as a result, was blacklisted by the FBI and obliged to emigrate to Canada.

AVANT GARDE

The magazine *Avant Garde* (left) was founded in 1968 and was in its own words 'exuberantly' dedicated to the future'. It gave Herb Lubalin a platform to tackle taboo subjects such as sex and drugs, using iconoclastic typography with a (then compulsory) touch of psychedelia.

a surrealist fantasy world, with homages to Art Nouveau and period advertising. Type was often kinetic and wilfully illegible – a legacy later taken up by the punk and techno generations.

In Britain, flower power and hippy culture spread like wildfire, and Carnaby Street became a byword for fashion and flamboyance. Michael English's pop-art designs were everywhere, and in 1968, Richard Avedon immortalized the Beatles in hand-coloured solarized photographs.

But the climate of change was not limited to the field of culture. Resistance to the Vietnam War inspired Tomi Ungerer's 'Kiss for Peace' and 'Black Power, White Power', and fuelled a wave of protest and demonstration in America, exemplified by the Berkeley Free Press. In Europe, the same spirit fired the Provos in Amsterdam (also influenced by the International Situationists) and the students and workers on the streets of French cities in May 1968. The Atelier Populaire produced a stream of posters, often monochrome and silkscreen-printed, minimalist images with striking slogans that became icons of the protest movement. A number of these student artists

Distributed in its hundreds of thousands with a Bob Dylan album, this portrait (above) by Milton Glaser, with its pop-art hair, remains a classic design from a period that saw a boom in this kind of decorative image.

UNIVERSITÉ POPULAIRE

OUI

Left, French poster from the student protests of May 1968.

were inspired by Cuba, where posters by Félix Beltrán and René Azcuy were using strong colour, simple images and powerful slogans. And above all they looked to Poland, home to a school of design that was unique in the genre.

Innovations in eastern Europe

Poland had been a centre of intense activity in graphic design since before the war, and this continued post-war in the work of artists such as Tadeusz Trepkowski and Eryk H. Lipinski. Its influence spread primarily through the teachings of two key figures at the Warsaw Academy of Fine Arts: Henryk Tomaszewski and Josef Mroszczak. Mroszczak was also art director of WAG, the state agency that commissioned film posters, and in 1966 he founded the Warsaw Biennale. Tomaszewski's work was influential in passing on the uninhibited use of symbolism, conceptualism and colour, using hand-drawn lettering that playfully thumbed its nose at methodical systems of typography. Poland was unique among socialist countries in producing a galaxy of artists and designers working in highly individual styles: Lenica and Cieslewicz (perhaps the most dramatic, who later turned to photography); the fantasy-surrealists Starowieyski, Majewski and Czerniawski; the symbolist Wiktor Gorka; Waldemar Swierzy with his portraits of jazz musicians; and Jan Mlodozeniec, with his bold colours and outlines. The list could go on, with Palka, Urbaniec and others. Through the pages of *Projekt* magazine, the influence of the Polish school spread throughout the world, with its more personal emphasis hinting at the individual behind the design. Eventually, however, this could not survive without state support, which was crucially lacking after the fall of the Iron Curtain.

Militants and independents

It was in continental Europe that – against all the odds – independent and for the most part politically militant

Surrealist fantasy was the hallmark of many posters of the Polish school, often marked by a streak of violent and macabre imagery. Above, poster by Jan Lenica for the opera *Wozzeck*, 1964; opposite, film poster by Franciszek Starowieyski for *The Hourglass Sanatorium*, 1973.

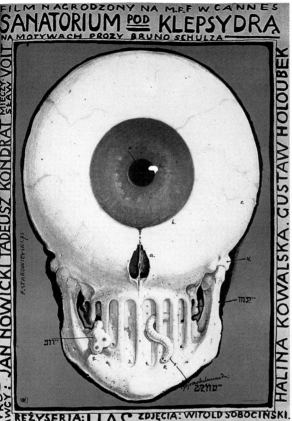

By contrast, Henryk Tomaszewski used a minimalist style and almost no words to capture the quintessence of graphic design (poster opposite, top). His influence on the generations of designers he taught at the Warsaw Academy of Fine Arts made his contribution all the more significant.

•If one day we were asked to answer the question "What is graphic art?", any reply would have to be as equivocal as Hamlet's. In my modest opinion, it begins with the petroglyphs of Central Asia and ends with the signs of Henryk Tomaszewski. There is no point in listing all his colleagues and activists of this century, Henryk's students or fans. I believe Tomaszewski is unique because he embodies the basic, the beautiful and the useful. Highly public and deeply private, prudish and poetic, his work does not tell a story: it makes a statement. This is the truth as I see it: Henryk Tomaszewski is great, and without him the world of poster design would have been a sadder one.•

Roman Cieslewicz,
Henryk Tomaszewski,
1995

graphic design managed to survive. Young and socially committed (at least to begin with), many of these designers rejected the world of advertising, and instead found refuge in working for public services and state-subsidized cultural activities, including theatre, opera, museums and festivals. They were also teachers, passing on their commitment to a new generation of designers.

The model for this approach was the Grapus design collective, founded in Paris in 1970 by Pierre Bernard, François Miehe and Gérard Paris-Clavel. Trained by Tomaszewski in Poland, this trio were also united by

the formative experience of May 1968; Miehe soon left, however, while Jean-Paul Bachollet and Alex Jordan joined the collective. Grapus produced work for the French Communist Party (notably for the Festival of Humanity and the CGT union movement) until they were ousted for being too reckless, and for small independent theatres such as the TEP, the Odéon and the Théâtre de la Salamandre, for whom they produced publicity material and posters that were classics of their type, startling in their acuteness and originality. They were also involved in many demonstrations and protests for the socialist cause.

Overflowing with creativity and colour, manipulating old photographs and using them in juxtaposition or montages, with hand-drawn lettering that leapt off the paper with exhilarating freedom, their work (like the revolution they espoused) was new, fresh and impossible to ignore. Spending time working with the Grapus collective became almost a rite of passage for an entire generation of designers, such as Annick Orliange, who later produced work for Paris's Banlieues Bleues festival. Michel Quarez, an older designer who had worked in advertising (at the agency SNIP) and was briefly a member of the group, contributed a warmth and faux-naif charm with his childlike drawings and luminous use of colour. Working for local councils in the Paris

These two posters (left and opposite) both belong to the same stylistic and political ethos. In each, the effect relies on exaggeration: for the Festival of Humanity, Grapus intensifies the red of the flag shown floating against a blue sky. Quarez, meanwhile, gives a huge red hand to the little figure greeting his neighbour. Both designs are characterized by a strong, simple concept; direct, crudely drawn images; liberal expanses of colour; and hand-drawn, uninhibited lettering.

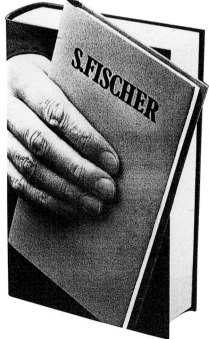

suburbs, Quarez produced campaigns that promoted neighbourliness with simplicity and gentle humour.

This first generation of committed designers produced two other outstanding figures. Alain Le Quernec, another former student of Tomaszewski, successfully rose to the challenge of introducing good graphic design to his native Brittany. Brimming over with ideas, from pop art to manipulated photography, his images became inextricably linked with the region's identity, not only in the cultural sphere but also in the field of social issues such as campaigns against oil pollution and nuclear power. Michel Bouvet, finally, graduated from the Beaux-Arts in 1978 and went to work for the Maison de la Culture in Créteil, before moving on to clients ranging from the Charleville Puppet Festival to several major French theatre companies.

Germany was not to be left behind: Klaus Staeck, associated with Fluxus and Joseph Beuys, denounced the political system with photomontages of raw and shocking violence, using his own unorthodox distribution system to put more than twenty million copies of his work into print. Gunter Rambow trained in Kassel before moving to Frankfurt and setting up Studio Rambow with Gerhard Lienemeyer and Michael van de Sand. Although he did some political work (notably for Germany's Green Party), he was active for the most part

Although he is politically committed and has designed posters for the German Green Party, the German designer Gunter Rambow also undertakes regular commissions in the private sector, producing distinguished work for the theatre and publishing. His series of montages for the publisher Fischer (opposite below) displays his remarkable photographic talents. Stripped of all superfluous detail, his posters are consummately legible and have an inescapable dramatic intensity. In work such as this, Rambow achieves a conciseness that is beyond words and that may well be the logical conclusion of all graphic art: images that speak for themselves.

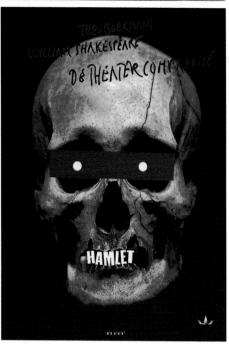

in the cultural arena. An
outstanding photographer,
Rambow created classic
campaigns for the Frankfurt
Theatre and montages for the
publisher Fischer. He was also
responsible for all packaging
and presentation for Hessische Rundfunk. Constantly
reinventing his style, he reached the ultimate in graphic
symbolism, using a maximum of two or three colours,
for the Wiesbaden Theatre.

Heinz Edelmann carried out a great deal of work
for the Westdeutscher Rundfunk and the Theater der
Welt in Essen, always with wry humour and a gleeful
style; Uwe Loesch's designs for the Düsseldorfer
Kom(m)ödchen cabaret and the Ruhrlandmuseum in
Essen were in a dramatically opposed style, minimalist
and mysterious. Pierre Mendell and Klaus Oberer
produced posters for the Bavarian Opera; Frieder
Grindler worked in Stuttgart, Otto Stein almost
everywhere. In the East, Volker Pfüller carried on a long
tradition of Expressionist theatre posters in Berlin, while
also training students such as Henning Wagenbreth and
Anke Feuchtenberger; Felix Büttner, meanwhile, was
working in Rostock. After years spent designing an

•The first image that
came to me was the
caustic laughter of the
father toying with the
son who does not
understand.•

Anthon Beeke on his
poster for *Hamlet*
(above)

Heinz Edelmann
has worked for
German radio (WDR)
for many years, using
gentle humour such as
the man with the big ear
(above left) to imprint
his visual jokes on the
public's memory.

The theatre remains one of the last refuges of independent graphic designers wanting to work in the cultural arena (far left, poster by Holger Matthies). Many Western European countries have seen a proliferation of both national and regional theatre companies , offering creative opportunities not only for poster design but also for programmes and company branding. Classics such as *Hamlet* are revived again and again, each time inspiring new and different ideas.

unparalleled series of cinema posters, Holger Matthies also turned to the theatre, in Frankfurt and Berlin. The world of jazz, finally, found its appointed designer for the festivals of both Frankfurt and Berlin in Günther Kieser.

Resisting the commonplace

Switzerland boasted equally remarkable designers. Each worked in his own region: Paul Brühwiler in Zurich, Odermatt and Tissi between Zurich and Lucerne, Claude Kuhn-Klein in Berne, Werner Jecker and Pierre Neumann in Lausanne, and Roger Pfund in Geneva. All produced work that was highly artistic in style. And in the middle of nowhere – or more accurately in the small town of Willisau – Niklaus Troxler founded a jazz festival that soon became world-famous, for which he designed a series of vibrantly coloured and constantly varied posters. Ralph Schraivogel used superimposed photography for the Zurich film festival in ways that were wholly original.

In the Netherlands, Jan van Torn carried on Willem Sandberg's anarchic approach and Swip Stolk launched his baroque pop-art style, but two other designers were unquestionably the dominant figures in the field: Gert Dumbar, who, alongside his highly disciplined photographic and typographical projects, was also able to free himself from all constraints and produce work of unstructured exuberance such as his designs for the

Niklaus Troxler (poster above right) is a unique artist whose work in the world of jazz music is exceptional. He and his brother began to run a jazz festival in their small hometown of Willisau in Switzerland in 1975, and ever since then he has been the most prolific and talented of jazz poster artists. The fact that none of the world's major jazz festivals have produced anything that can compare with his posters speaks volumes. Troxler still works tirelessly in a field that he has made his own.

Netherlands Festival; and the pugnacious and Falstaffian figure of Anthon Beeke, whose carnal obsessions and colourful imagination were expressed in commissions from a wide range of clients.

All over Europe, graphic designers chose to specialize in the cultural arena rather than yielding to the triteness and constraints of the advertising industry. Festivals were their natural milieu, and many of them were members of the AGI (Alliance Graphique Internationale). In Barcelona, the multi-talented Peret was equally at home with sculpture as with poster design; Mariscal created Cobi, mascot of the Barcelona Olympics, and moved seamlessly from strip cartoons to interior design. Italy boasted the typographic genius of Bruno Monguzzi and the elegance of Italo Lupi; Hungary had Peter Pocs; Finland, Kari Piippo; Denmark, Per Arnoldi; Croatia, Boris Bucan; and Russia, the late Iurii Bokser.

The Japanese revelation

In the late 1970s, the arrival of the Japanese in the essentially fairly closed world of high-quality graphic design came like a revelation – or rather an unfurling, for the images revealed were not only totally original and of the highest quality but were also as varied as the artists who created them were numerous. In the early 1950s, followers of graphic design had already admired posters by Yusaku Kamekura (Nikon), and elegant compositions by Ikko Tanaka. Posters for the Tokyo Olympics in 1964, featuring photographs and text laid out with faultless confidence by Kamekura, were the first examples of Japanese graphic design to receive worldwide publicity.

Two powerful institutions, the JAGDA (Japanese Graphic Designers' Association) with its forerunner the JAAC (Japan Adverting Artists' Club), founded in 1951 with Kamekura as its president, and Nippon Design Center under its director Kazumasa Nagai, developed

At first glance, Kamekura, whose posters for the Tokyo Olympics (below) revealed a talent for graphic design of the highest order, and Yokoo, who the following year designed his *A la maison de M. Civeçawa* poster for the

Au Ku Ko Buto Ha avant-garde theatre group, seem to have little in common. Nonetheless, both were pioneers of Japanese graphic design, which had no dominant style but rather a combination of strong personalities, all of whom had to find an original style in order to make their mark.

'Cobi [mascot of the Barcelona Olympics in 1992, created by Mariscal] appeared on over 600 different objects, manufactured by 58 licensed companies. The price he fetched varied between 50 and 100,000 pesetas, according to whether he appeared on a stickpin, or a piece of jewelry, a comic strip or a fast-food wrapper, a postage stamp, a banknote, a piece of sculpture, a silkscreen print, a T-shirt, or even on an inflatable swimming pool. He could be found in every possible location, reproduced by every possible technique and on every possible type of object.'

Llàtzer Moix,
Mariscal à Paris, 1994

in step with Japan's flourishing economy, with its cutting-edge technology that was poised to conquer the world. At the same time, the Japanese were emerging from the hardships of years of reconstruction and discovering – with fervent enthusiasm – the consumer society and cosmopolitan influences from all over the world. It was in this context that graphic design in Japan simply exploded. Alongside Kamekura, master of modernist classicism, and Tanaka, with his elegantly poised reworkings of traditional culture, there now appeared Tadanori Yokoo, the first Japanese designer with the ability to startle all and sundry. Adapting pop

art to Japanese tastes and using brilliant colours, he combined fragments of Japanese popular imagery with references culled from eclectic sources (such as Ingres's *Le Bain Turc*) which he mixed up, overlaid and used to make collages. The effect was extraordinary. Having gone through psychedelic and 'Bad Painting' periods, he has now returned to his early style. His huge volume of work includes book covers, magazine illustrations (with portraits making reference to the tradition of *ukiyo-e* prints), and posters that exhausted all available technical possibilities. Active at the same time as Yokoo, in the mid-1970s, Kiyoshi Awazu produced designs in a highly coloured pop-art style based on flowing, organic forms. In a diametrically different approach, Shigeo Fukuda's work made heavy use of optical illusions.

Following the example of Makoto Nakamura (poster above left), Eiko Ishioka – who preferred to work in black and white (opposite above) – also started out working for Shiseido, as did Shin Matsunaga (canned vegetables, opposite below).

Above, interactive two-monthly calendars designed for Shiseido in 1998 by John Maeda.

There was a logical inevitability about the Japanese being the first to experiment with computer art: Mitsuo Katsui was the pioneer in the field, followed by the bizarre spatial compositions of Kasumasa Nagai who, displaying the disconcerting ease with which the Japanese switch styles, then devoted himself to a bestiary of stylized animals; tradition and modernity being two basic elements of Japanese art. All these artists worked for national festivals and exhibitions in Japan, as well as carrying out prestigious campaigns for major advertising clients and publishers.

This variety was another feature specific to Japanese graphic design: while Makoto Nakamura revolutionized cosmetics advertising with his close-up photos for Shiseido, Eiko Ishioka, art director of Parco, the youth brand of Seibu department stores, was making daring use of every technique from illustration to photography. In Japan it was understood that traditional images and the mere presentation of merchandise would not attract the attention of a young audience. Young people needed to be lured and startled by images of a parallel universe of crazy extravagance. Their response was not rational and objective, but emotional and subjective: Masatoshi Toda's surrealist images for the Vivre department store, Katsumi Asaba's masterly typography, and above all Makoto Saito's photomontages for the stores Batsu and Alpha Cubic, in which he gave free rein to one of the greatest visual imaginations of his generation.

Abandoning themselves to these delirious images of consumerism and fashion, Japanese designers took little interest in the public domain, with only Masuteru Aoba

•The images of beautiful women produced by Shiseido…are the embodiment of contemporary female beauty. Because of this, advertising campaigns may today be considered as having artistic or cultural value.… The Shiseido posters, and especially those created by Makoto Nakamura, may be viewed as *ukiyo-e* images of contemporary female beauty.•

Kazumasa Nagai

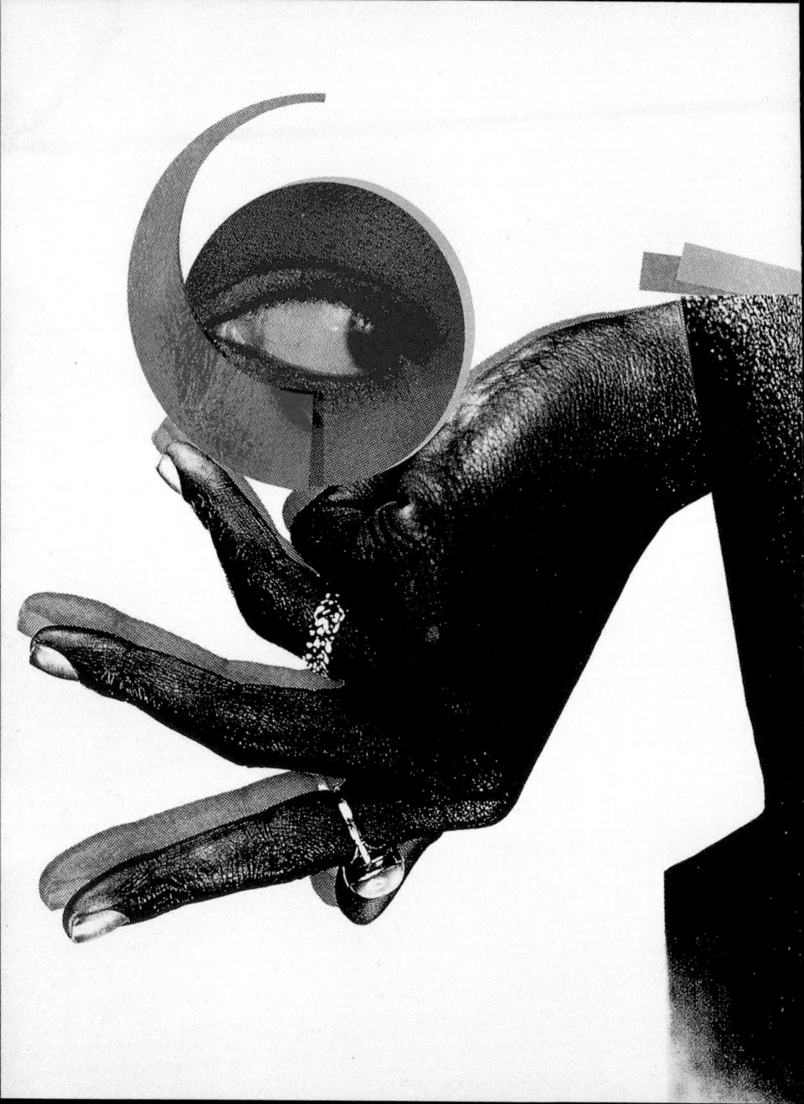

Makoto Saito's work in fashion and the media since the early 1980s, highly versatile in style but with a predilection for photomontage, demonstrates the remarkable power of this great Japanese designer's imagination. He lays out his virtually text-free compositions (here for Virgin) without the aid of a computer (he has been called a 'low tech' designer), and without always knowing exactly what the end product will be. Indeed he positively relishes the accidental and the unexpected. The result: extraordinary images of undiluted originality which take a wholly Japanese approach and touch the public's emotions. 'Ten people looking at my poster might see ten different things', observes this extravagantly imaginative designer.

and U. G. Sato (protesting against French atomic testing on Mururoa Atoll) working in this arena. Supported by businesses with a major tradition of excellence in graphic design, and served by printers of remarkable skill, Japanese graphic design is now an undisputed leader in the field.

Computers and graphic design

The finest graphic designers working in the 1980s all displayed virtuoso levels of skill in draughtsmanship and photography, and all (including, according to his own writings, Makoto Saito) saw computers as useful practical tools in the final stages of their work. But with the appearance of the

Apple Mac in the same decade, there came to the fore a generation of designers who considered it as a natural creative tool, particularly for typography. Most of these young designers belonged to the music business and this was the field in which they did most of their work. Nevertheless, some of the most talented were recruited by major advertisers, including Nike, who quickly realized that this was the visual vocabulary of their target market. Music and video themselves were in the throes of the same technological revolution as graphic design. In under a decade, technology made greater advances than in the whole of the previous century. The technical

°It looks as though there's a plug in the man's mouth [above] .... With the choice of colours, I wanted to undermine danger in the same way that big conglomerates package their products with soothing colours.°
Neville Brody

Logo (left) and Some Bizarre/Virgin Records album cover (above) for the band Cabaret Voltaire, 1984, by Neville Brody.

perfection of offset litho and photo-typesetting, and the invention of Letraset in 1960 had already brought about huge changes in design, but the arrival of the computer was a genuine revolution. With the rapid appearance of software such as Aldus Pagemaker, Quark Xpress, Adobe Illustrator and Photoshop, along with ever more powerful hardware, computers became omnipresent. Gradually these disrupted, altered or replaced the entire production process by which graphic design had traditionally operated, from the delivery of the commission to the printing of the final product.

It all started in London, with Jamie Reid's collages and 'in-your-face' images for the Sex Pistols and the audacious though all too brief career of Barney Bubbles

•You want to encourage people to read an article. You have to indicate where each article starts. But the way you start an article can take any form you like, as long as you're still indicating the beginning by directing the reader's eye to it. You can use a symbol, a form or a different typeface; you might even use white space; you can use any means.•
Neville Brody

(working name of Colin Fulcher). It seemed that music was everywhere.

Neville Brody started out designing record sleeves and publicity material for Fetish Records and the band Cabaret Voltaire. Like many of the designers who sprung from the music business, his references were a combination of Dada and Fluxus, and he found his inspiration in the work of Andy Warhol, Marcel Duchamp, John Cage, William S. Burroughs, Allen Ginsberg and the Beat Generation. In 1981 Brody

Above, double-page spread with headline bleeding onto the previous page by Neville Brody from *The Face*, issue 42, October 1983 became art director of *The Face* magazine, moving to *Arena* in 1986. Even before the computer age, Brody had grasped the need for a new approach to typography and the urgency of finding a vocabulary that the target market – in this case young people – would understand. His work was influential throughout the world. Pursuing his passion for typography, he founded *Fuse* and set up the Research Studio and, with MetaDesign, FontShop, which diffused his ideas and images worldwide. With Peter Saville's esoteric images for Dindisc Records, London now set the tone. Meanwhile Amsterdam, another capital city of the music business, had since the early 1980s been dominated by Hard Werken and Mark Kisman, who challenged Dutch typography with his work for *Vinyl* magazine.

'The sense lies far in the background'

April Greiman, now returned from Basel, began work in the United States. The giant image that she produced, with the photographer Jayme Odgers, for the Los Angeles Olympics was uninhibited and lyrical in style, but it was in 1986 that she created her first truly computer-generated design, for a special issue of *Design Quarterly*: a two-metre long, fold-out image of herself, naked amid a chaotic cocktail of text and images. To the question, 'Does it make sense?', Greiman offers an answer borrowed from Wittgenstein: 'There is a picture in the foreground, but the sense lies far in the

⁶Much of the scepticism and disfavour currently attached to digital images will disappear as a new generation of designers enters the profession. Having grown-up with computers at home and school, these designers will assimilate computer technology into the visual communication process as it penetrates everyday practices. With computers, designers will be able to personally control their work to an unprecedented degree, from designing custom typefaces to editing colour separations. This will surely increase the specialization of the profession. But it will, above all, extend the creative process into previously unexplored areas.⁹

Emigre, 'The New Primitives', *I.D.*, 1988 (promotional posters for *Emigre*, opposite above, and typeface design, opposite below right)

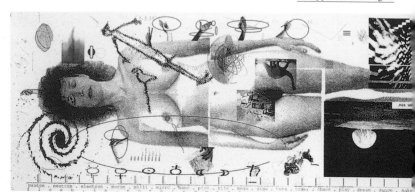

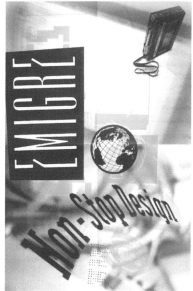

background.' In her work, form and content are always inseparable. This would also clearly be the key to all forms of communication to come: for all those whom Massimo Vignelli, keeper of the Swiss tradition, described as working in the 'Garbage Style', legibility was simply not a problem; an image created in a specific context for a specific public could ignore the canons of international typography with impunity.

Founded in Berkeley by designer Rudy VanderLans and typographer Zuzana Licko, *Emigre* magazine was a trailblazer of digital typography, using typefaces designed by Licko and others such as Edward Fella. It came up with radical ideas such as 'creating a font virus that would transform every Helvetica into something much more

What you see
What you see
What you see
What you see
What you see

●A sheet of paper isn't merely a neutral receiver of symbols, but a field of space that is traversed. The eye walks, jumps, journeys through, inside and outside of it.●
April Greiman
(opposite, fold-out poster for *Design Quarterly*, 1986)

desirable – the post-modern typographer's revenge.'
Very soon, it attracted the attentions of digital design
fanatics, mostly self-taught and comprehensively
iconoclastic in outlook. Two of them expressed their
views in issue 15: Jeffery Keedy stated that 'I don't see
our role at all as forcing a change on communication.
Communication is always in flux.' Barry Deck,
meanwhile was even more categorical:
'I am really interested in type that isn't
perfect. Type that reflects more truly the
imperfect language of an imperfect world
inhabited by imperfect beings.'

The third key figure was David Carson.
After studying sociology he became a
surfer, which in 1988 led to his becoming
art director of *Beach Culture*. From there
he moved to *Ray Gun* ('new music/new
digital typography'), where his eccentric
typography won an enthusiastic following.
Often he used the text to create images into
which he would insert an eclectic range
of visuals. Carson gave physical form to
Marshall MacLuhan's famous words: here
the medium really was the message.

Reflecting on Carson's influence, David
Byrne observed, 'Print will no longer be
obliged to simply carry the news. It will
have been given (or will have taken, in this
case) its freedom, and there is
no going back. Print is reborn,
resurrected, as something
initially unrecognizable. It's
not really dead, it simply
mutated into something else.'
Carson's success and influence
were huge and he assumed cult
status – and was poached by
the major advertisers.

Movements or individuals?

'Movement' is a misnomer
in this context, as all these

Ed Fella, professor at the California Institute of the Arts and former ad designer, used an anti-aesthetic approach to create a new aesthetic. His series of conference posters (below) were like bombs

thrown into the conventions of typography and design.

Paula Scher, who joined Pentagram in 1992, brought an uninhibited approach to her work for the Public Theater (left). Working outside the normal conventions, she created a kind of 'street typography', similar in spirit to graffiti.

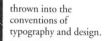

designers were ferociously individualistic, even to the point of anonymity in the vogue for flyers of the early 1990s, but it is still possible to distinguish two generations. First of the founding generation was Paula Scher, who started her career in the early 1970s as art director of CBS, created pastiches of Herbert Matter posters for Swatch in 1985, then produced increasingly

David Carson, a cult figure to a whole generation of young designers, was another typographer who tore up the rule book and threw it away. It was in the world of surfing that he created his system of

experimental work for the Public Theater. Tibor Kalman produced a video for Talking Heads in 1988 in which type played a major part. Closer to its American roots, Art Chantry, chronicler of pop culture, and Ed Fella who, after what he described as thirty years of 'semi-vernacular' practice in advertising, embarked on the wildest experimental work. There were also several influential French designers including Pierre di Sciullo, who founded *Qui résiste?* in 1983, Philippe Apeloig, who in 1989 designed the 'Typographic Age' cover for *Emigre*, and Fabien Baron, the creative director of *Harper's Bazaar*, who in 1992 designed Madonna's controversial book *Sex*.

cut-outs, overlaps and distortions: in the image above, the typography evokes the thrilling dangers of 'the big one'. Bored by the platitudes of an ad industry that was out of step with their aspirations, young people were quick to respond – and advertisers such as Nike, Pepsi, MTV and Sony were equally quick to catch on.

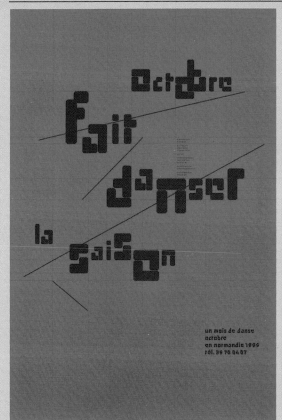

octobre
fait
danser
la saison

un mois de danse
octobre
en normandie 1999
tél. 39 70 04 07

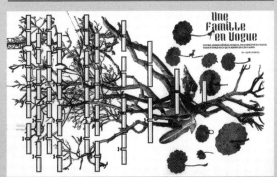

Une Famille
en Vogue

While Philippe Apeloig (poster, left) believed that 'one of the chief natural habitats for graphic designers is cultural communication', often in conjunction with teaching, other designers had very different ideas. French duo M/M, for instance (posters above and below left), came to prominence with their work for the Théâtre de Lorient, moved from the music business (Björk) into fashion (Sitbon, Yamamoto), then even worked for the Centre Pompidou with artists such as Philippe Parreno and Pierre Huyghe. Meanwhile, Laurent Fétis (poster for Beck, opposite), declared 'I do not feel that I am heir to a specifically French culture.' Although he has continued to work in Paris on a regular basis, notably for the Musée d'Art Moderne, his client base is worldwide, and includes the music business and cutting-edge magazines.

However marginal the music business might appear, along with its fallout in the world of fashion, it nevertheless established a reciprocal relationship with the big advertising studios: Designers' Republic, founded in London by Ian Anderson in 1986, moved from comic strips to photographic manipulation, in the process producing a copy of the Pepsi logo for the band Pop Will Eat Itself that sailed very close to infringing copyright laws. In Japan their work with clients such as Nike and Sony caused a sensation.

In the wake of Jean Lagarrigue and Jean-Paul Goude, Fabien Baron became creative director of *Harper's Bazaar* in New York in 1992. He also runs his own agency, creating

Just Design in New York worked for Sire, Warner Music, Sony and Polygram, as well as for major performers such as Lou Reed; Post Tool, who used computer graphics like no one else, specialized in three-dimensional work; Why Not Associates, founded in 1987 by students of Gert Dumbar, produced delirious images for Virgin Records, CBS and Smirnoff. Vaughn Oliver, another British trailblazer, left the 4AD label to start 1/23. Also in London, a group of experimental musicians, painters and video makers got together to form the Tomato collective. As well as working for Nike and Levi's, they designed the title sequence for the film *Trainspotting*. Stefan Sagmeister left Tibor Kalman's studio to produce images that were both ironic and provocative. All these designers and their computer-generated images embody the vitality of contemporary graphic design – which is to be found, as may clearly be seen, wherever life is lived.

striking campaigns for fashion houses such as Balenciaga (above), Calvin Klein and Armani.

It is impossible within the context of a work such as this to list all the best graphic designers working today, all the more so since the advent of computer graphics has increased their numbers while at the same time making them less visible. They can be found in the pages of

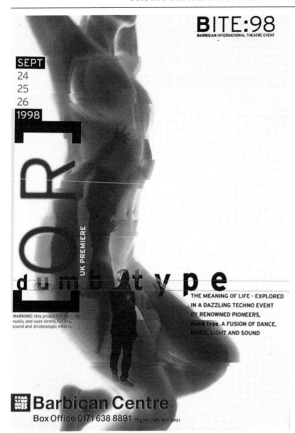

BITE:98
BARBICAN INTERNATIONAL THEATRE EVENT

SEPT
24
25
26
1998

[OR]

UK PREMIERE

d u m b t y p e

THE MEANING OF LIFE - EXPLORED
IN A DAZZLING TECHNO EVENT
BY RENOWNED PIONEERS,
dumb type. A FUSION OF DANCE,
MUSIC, LIGHT AND SOUND

WARNING: this production features
nudity and uses strong lighting,
sound and stroboscopic effects.

Barbican Centre
Box Office 0171 638 8891 Bkg fee (9am-8pm daily)

'If I were asked by another businessperson for one piece of advice on how to succeed, it would be this: make certain that your designer knows the audience you want to reach, then heed what he or she has to say, even if it is a bit scary and means stretching beyond the known. Think of the designer as someone who can bring value to your effort. If you view your designer only as a vendor, that is the kind of output you will get. If you consider your designer a partner in your business, you're a lot farther along the road to achieving your goals. So let the critics call what we produce Radical. I call it good business sense. And I call it exciting. That, to me, is a lot more important than maintaining the status quo.'
Marvin Scott-Jarrett, founder of *Ray Gun* magazine

A bove, poster by Why Not Associates, 1998. Overleaf, Stefan Sagmeister, poster for the album *Set the Twilight Reeling* by Lou Reed, 1998.

magazines such as *Eye* or *Creative Review* in London, *Idea* in Tokyo, *Print Graphics* in New York or *Etapes Graphiques* in France – to name only the best-known titles. What really matters is that fashion, the music business and the internet have between them removed graphic design from the ghetto of public service and high culture, where sadly the demand for its services has often stagnated. Perhaps the time has come for graphic design to move closer once again to the world that it has served since its birth: the world of business and industry.

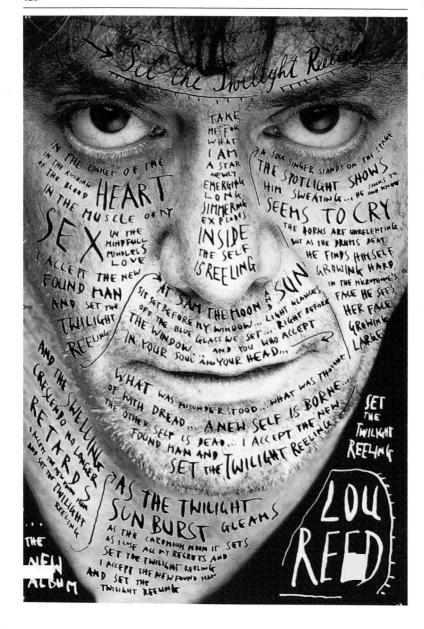

DOCUMENTS

Early writings on graphic design

Graphic artists have always had strong ideas about the aims of their profession and the best way to achieve the highest possible quality in their work. This selection ranges from William Morris's concepts of craftsmanship and true beauty in typography to A. M. Cassandre's poetic evocation of the rise of advertising.

William Morris: 'the most harmonious decoration possible'

I began printing books with the hope of producing some which would have a definite claim to beauty, while at the same time they should be easy to read and should not dazzle the eye, or trouble the intellect of the reader by eccentricity of form in the letters. I have always been a great admirer of the calligraphy of the Middle Ages, and of the earlier printing which took its place. As to the fifteenth-century books, I had noticed that they were always beautiful by force of the mere typography, even without the added ornament, with which many of them are so lavishly supplied. And it was the essence of my undertaking to produce books which it would be a pleasure to look upon as pieces of printing and arrangement of type. Looking at my adventure from this point of view then, I found I had to consider chiefly the following things: the paper, the form of the type, the relative spacing of the letters, the words, and the lines; and lastly the position of the printed matter on the page.

...By instinct rather than by conscious thinking it over, I began by getting myself a fount of Roman type. And here what I wanted was letter pure in form; severe, without needless excrescences; solid, without the thickening and thinning of the line, which is the essential fault of the ordinary modern type, and which makes it difficult to read; and not compressed laterally, as all later type has grown to be owing to commercial exigencies. There was only one source from which to take examples of this perfected Roman type, to wit, the works of the great Venetian printers of the fifteenth century, of whom Nicholas Jenson produced the completest and most Roman characters from 1470 to 1476. This type I studied with much care, getting it photographed to a big scale, and drawing it over many times before I began designing my own letter; so that though I think I mastered the essence of it, I did not copy it servilely; in fact, my Roman type, especially in the lower case, tends rather more to the Gothic than does Jenson's.

After a while I felt that I must have a Gothic as well as a Roman fount; and herein the task I set myself was to redeem the Gothic character from the charge of unreadableness which is commonly brought against it.... Keeping my end steadily in view, I designed a black-letter type which I think I may claim to be as readable as a Roman one, and to say the truth I prefer it to the Roman. This type is of the size called Great Primer (the Roman type is of 'English' size); but later on I was driven by the necessities of the Chaucer (a double-columned book) to get a smaller Gothic type of Pica size.

...Now as to the spacing: First, the 'face' of the letter should be as nearly conterminous with the 'body' as possible, so as to avoid undue whites between the letters. Next, the lateral spaces between the words should be (a) no more than is necessary to distinguish clearly the division into words, and (b) should be as nearly equal as possible. Modern printers, even the best, pay very

should always leave the inner margin the narrowest, the top somewhat wider, the outside (fore-edge) wider still, and the bottom widest of all. This rule is never departed from in mediaeval books, written or printed. Modern printers systematically transgress against it; thus apparently contradicting the fact that the unit of a book is not one page, but a pair of pages. A friend, the librarian of one of our most important private libraries, tells me that after careful testing he has come to the conclusion that the mediaeval rule was to make a difference of 20 per cent from margin to margin. Now these matters of spacing and position are of the greatest importance in the production of beautiful books; if they are properly considered they will make a book

UNE LETTRE N'EST **RIEN**

little heed to these two essentials of seemly composition, and the inferior ones run riot in licentious spacing, thereby producing, inter alia, those ugly rivers of lines running about the page which are such a blemish to decent printing. Third, the whites between the lines should not be excessive; the modern practice of 'leading' should be used as little as possible, and never without some definite reason, such as marking some special piece of printing. The only leading I have allowed myself is in some cases a 'thin' lead between the lines of my Gothic pica type: in the Chaucer and the double-columned books I have used a 'hair' lead, and not even this in the 16mo books. Lastly, but by no means least, comes the position of the printed matter on the page. This

printed in quite ordinary type at least decent and pleasant to the eye. The disregard of them will spoil the effect of the best designed type.

It was only natural that I, a decorator by profession, should attempt to ornament my books suitably: about this matter, I will only say that I have always tried to keep in mind the necessity for making my decoration a part of the page of type. I may add that in designing the magnificent and inimitable woodcuts which have adorned several of my books, and will above all adorn the Chaucer which is now drawing near completion, my friend Sir Edward Burne-Jones has never lost sight of this important point, so that his work will not only give us a series of most beautiful and imaginative pictures, but form the most harmonious decoration possible to the printed book.

William Morris, 'A Note on His Aims in Founding the Kelmscott Press', published in *Modern Art*, 1896

The poster – a vulgar art?

...The truth is that the artistic and non-artistic views of 'vulgarity', as entertained by the English people, are sharply at variance. The vulgarity of the non-artistic poster rarely strikes them: but in the artistic – almost exclusively in the treatment of the feminine figure – what they call vulgarity is usually a certain suggestiveness, usually fancied, rarely real, which in either case the artist hardly notices, if at all, on account of its artistry.

'I fear,' says Mr Walter Crane, in discussing the matter from another point of view, 'that there is something essentially vulgar about the idea of a poster unless it is limited to simple announcements or directions, or becomes a species of heraldry, or sign-painting. The jostling together of conflicting scenes and motives on the hoarding, however, to which all must submit, is as inartistic a condition of things as a picture exhibition. The very fact of the necessity of shouting loud, and the association with vulgar commercial puffing, are against the artist and so much dead weight.'

But, surely, the fact is at last becoming recognized that 'shouting' is no longer necessary. Just as to practised ears in a boiler-shop the whisper of a man or a soft note of music can be heard above the deafening din of a hundred hammers, so the artistic poster of real beauty proclaims itself gently, but irresistibly, out of the mass of violent kaleidoscopic colour and common design. Few colours in strong contrast

skilfully arranged, the fewest lines and masses, simple chiaroscuro, added to charm, grace, dignity, or vigour of design – these are the elements and essentials: and if the conditions are properly fulfilled, the result is an artistic triumph of which any artist might be proud. That we in England, too long delayed, are at last advancing toward this point, there is little reason to doubt: not, primarily, through any motives of philanthropy on the part of the designers who are the mainspring of the movement, but rather through the law of self-protection against the perpetrations of bygone days. In this laudable crusade, they are being slowly encouraged by some of the advertisers themselves, who are finding that they can attract more attention with novel and artistic posters than with shouting ugliness or rampant Philistinism....

M. H. Spielmann, 'Posters and Poster Designing in England', from *The Modern Poster*, London, 1895

Colour in poster design

In painting, colour is a means of uniting forms by noting different tones or by replacing thse tones by shades of local colour, while in poster-designing, colour lies emphasis on particular parts of the design in order to make it as prominent as possible. Of course this does not mean that a poster designer is allowed to neglect harmony of colours, which is to him as important as to an artist-painter, the whole difference being the fact that they use the same medium for different purposes. The poster having as its aim to attract attention, the use of colour is, naturally, modified to this specific purpose so that a poster-designer can use his palette in a much freer way than a painter. It is probably this liberty that accounts for the ignoring of the principal characteristics of colour by a great many contemporary poster-designers. The knowledge of the basic qualities of colour may help a designer to achieve great simplicity and even to allot to the shapes in his design the colour which belongs specifically to these shapes in that position. For there is certainly a strict analogy between shapes and colours, and if they are properly combined their effectiveness must increase. A poster-designer, who can use more frequently than a painter both shapes and colours in their unmodified or slightly changed state, can make full use of this simple analogy without accepting any ready-made formula and without any hindrance to his personal conception of his art. In fact, he must have at his disposal a great accumulation of shapes, and their corresponding colours, which he can use at any time in all their variations. And he cannot use them without knowing their properties, for art is not guessing. I do not mean to imply that the only way to design a poster is to sit with compasses and ruler in hand and think hard which shapes correspond and which are their proper colours; and merely accept without reserve the teaching of Lou-Tch'-Ai-Che, who said: 'Some consider it noble to have a method; others consider it noble not to have a method. Not to have method is bad; to stop entirely at method is worse still. One should at first observe rules severely, the change them in an intelligent way. The aim of possessing method is to seem finally as if one had no method.'

R. A. Stephens, from *The Art of the Poster,* ed. E. McKnight Kauffer, London, 1924

Cassandre on the 'machine for advertising'

....Just as it does not fit in museums or collections, advertising eludes judgment. It is rather like love: we do not judge it, we are subjected to it. It is no longer a game, but a natural phenomenon like night and day: one of the most beautiful consequences of the modern world, of life itself, even....

The poster is no longer a picture but is becoming a 'machine for advertising'. Catalogues, advertisements, illuminated signs, so many living objects that are now as much a part of our daily lives as the telephone and the typewriter.

The language of advertising has been born: only just, but it has been born. A whole generation of artists have found their most vibrant mode of expression within it. It is used to solve a thousand problems, psychological or technical. The materials, processes and techniques serve only to make this machine run. Typography, offset, lithography, engraving, photocopies, halftones and colour prints are its driving forces, far more so than any outdated aesthetic ideas.

In the factory, the presses run, the ink flows like a river, coating a thousand cylinders. Kilometres of paper, caught up by steel fingers, disappear white then re-emerge yellow, then red, then blue: the same dot, the same line, the same colour is reproduced in the same way, in the same place, millions and millions of times.

Outside the posters clamour, the loudhailers call, the shop windows blaze like music-hall stages, the Cadum soap baby smiles, and suddenly, the Eiffel Tower lights up from top to bottom.

A. M. Cassandre, preface for the album *Publicité*, Paris, 1929

Advertising: the mother of graphic design

Steven Heller is senior art director of the New York Times, *editor of the* AIGA *Journal of Graphic Design, professor at the School of Visual Arts, New York, and the author of many articles and books. Here he discusses the relationship between advertising and graphic design.*

The word 'advertising' like 'commercial art', makes graphic designers cringe. It signifies all that sophisticated contemporary graphic design, or rather visual communications, is not supposed to be. Advertising is the tool of capitalism, a con that persuades an unwitting public to consume and consume again. Graphic design, by contrast is an aesthetic and philosophical pursuit that communicates ideas. Advertising is cultural exploitation that transforms creative expression into crass propaganda. Graphic design is a cultural force that incorporates parallel worldviews. Advertising is hypnotically invasive. Graphic design makes no such claim.

Though graphic design as we know it originated in the late nineteenth century as a tool of advertising, any association today with marketing, advertising, or capitalism deeply undermines the graphic designer's self-image. Graphic design history is an integral part of advertising history, yet in most accounts of graphic design's origins advertising is virtually denied, or hidden behind more benign words such as 'publicity' and 'promotion'. This omission not only limits the discourse, but misrepresents the facts. It is time for graphic design historians, and designers generally, to remove the elitist prejudices that have perpetuated a biased history.

Graphic Design as Art

...The 1950s saw the beginnings of a schism between graphic and advertising design. Modern graphic design veered from mass advertising toward corporate and institutional communications and evolved into a rarefied practice decidedly more sophisticated than advertising design of the same period. Some advertising artist/designers were celebrated for individual achievement, but as Terry Smith writes, 'advertising designed primarily by an individual artist was becoming rare enough in the United States to be remarkable, exceptional, and expensive.' Over time such advertising luminaries as did exist – E. McKnight Kauffer and A. M. Cassandre being the prime examples – were detached from the history of advertising and made into heroes of graphic design.

A kind of sociocultural stratification began to distinguish the advertising designer from the graphic designer. Today, a common view among advertising people is that graphic designers simply 'do letterheads', while graphic designers scorn their advertising counterparts for being ignorant about type. Job or class distinctions have driven a wedge between graphic designers and advertising designers and graphic design history has perpetuated the schism. While cultural scholars, consumer theorists, and media critics have done considerable work on the social, political, and psychological role of advertising in American culture, their writings are rarely cited in graphic design literature, as if issues of consumerism and marketing have no bearing on the 'art' of graphic design. This omission can be traced back to formal prejudices.

The Formalist Lens

If advertising is the function, then graphic design is the form. As Dwiggins pointed out in *Layout in Advertising*, 'The advertising piece is not an end-product; it is an intermediate step in a process. The end-product of advertising is not [design] – it is sales.' Yet selling is an ignored aspect of the story contemporary graphic design historians choose to tell – after all, graphic designers are not salespeople but form-givers, which is perceived as a more culturally significant activity than being a mere advertising huckster. The problem is that an advertisement must be analyzed as a collaborative endeavor involving considerably more than just its graphics. So to avoid having to admit that graphic design has a subordinate role, the historical discourse has built up around graphic design as a formal endeavor. As if in art history, graphic designs are removed from their contexts, placed on pedestals, and examined under the formalist lens. Like the annual design WYSIWYG competitions in which work is judged entirely on how it looks, graphic design, history more

often than not focuses attention on style, manner, and structure rather than on the success or failure of a piece of work in the marketplace. The audience, which is rarely considered in formalist critiques of fine art, is likewise ignored in favor of aesthetic and sometimes philosophical or ideological considerations. This not only denies the public's role, but the client's as well.

Unheroic Artifacts

...Graphic designers have distanced themselves from advertising in the same way that children put as much space as possible between themselves and their parents. And, indeed, graphic design did develop its own characteristics. American advertising was originally copy-based and unresponsive to design, and though reformers like Calkins (and later Bill Bernbach) encouraged the seamless integration of works, pictures, and design, the copy, slogan, and jingle have been the driving forces. From the turn of the century, would-be journalists and novelists were recruited as copywriters, giving the field a certain faux literary cast. Eventually, advertising developed its own stereotypical professionals, who even today are distinct from graphic design professionals.

The tilting of the scales toward the copy-driven 'big idea' is one reason why advertising histories veer away from extensive analysis of graphic design. Another issue is quality as defined by the two fields – a great advertising campaign may not be exceptional graphic design, while a superb piece of graphic design

may mask a poor advertising campaign. The history of advertising is more interested in how Marlboro cigarettes tested a variety of trade characters before stumbling on the Marlboro Man as a symbol of manliness. While graphic design appears negligible in the cultural analysis of this campaign, understanding the relationship of this symbol (which is graphic design in the broadest sense) to the larger mythology provides insight into how the American myth was perpetuated.

As important as this long-running campaign is (and not just as an example of politically incorrect thinking), it has never been analyzed in graphic design history for its symbolic connotations. Though the Lucky Strike package designed by Raymond Loewy and the

demographics, and other pseudosciences – are less important to graphic design history, considerably more consumerist theory, media criticism, and even perceptual psychology would be useful in understanding the form and function of graphic design through the advertising lens. Likewise, aesthetic theories can be applied through the lens of design to put a visually bereft advertising history into clearer focus.

During the past decade there have been calls to develop new narratives and to readdress graphic design history through feminist, ethnic, racial, post-structuralist, and numerous other politically correct perspectives. There are many ways to slice a pie, but before unveiling too many subtexts, it is perhaps first useful

IMPRIME DES

VIOTS

Eve Cigarette package designed by Herb Lubalin and Ernie Smith are featured as design artifacts, the advertising campaigns that sold the designs have been ignored. Graphic design historians are prudishly selective in what they discuss. They base decisions on ideal formal attributes – what is inherently interesting from a design perspective. They write as though consumerism is wicked – us (the canon) versus them (the mass) underscores graphic design history. Yet by eliminating advertising, design history loses rich insights into visual culture....

Today, advertising is not totally ignored – many trade magazines cover it – but it is rarely integrated into the broader analysis of graphic design. While certain aspects of advertising – marketing,

to reconcile a mother and her child.

Advertising and graphic design have more in common than the postmodern trend for vernacularism (or the aestheticization of timeworn artifacts) reveals. Advertising and graphic design are equally concerned with selling, communication, and entertaining. To appreciate one, the other is imperative. But more important, if graphic design history does not expand to include advertising and other related studies, it will ultimately succumb to the dead-end thinking that will be the inevitable consequence of being arrested in a state of continual adolescence.

Steven Heller, 'Advertising: the Mother of Graphic Design', from *Eye*, no. 17, vol. 5, summer 1995

The future of graphic design?

Steven Heller speculates wittily about the future of graphic design – and designers – as he traces the changing perceptions of its role from the 1980s onwards. Stephan Bundi, meanwhile, examines the place of individuality and imagination in a digital age in which computers have taken over many of the designer's traditional tasks.

The Next Small Thing

Graphic design came of age in the 1990s. It was no longer the stepchild of mass media or cousin of art, and we as designers became sought-after, highly trained professionals, respected by business, acknowledged by culture, needed by society. We basked in our history, criticism and public relations. It took 80 years to become the Next Big Thing, but now at the height of our maturity, while enjoying the glow of our glory, we are being transformed into the Next Small Thing.

After all the work it took to become a fashionable field with visible accomplishments; after all the struggle to make a name for ourselves as generators of cultural profit; and after having ridden the crest of that God-given gift – the digital wave – graphic design is no longer the cat's miaow. In fact, some might say we are being covered over in the litter box of media culture.

Not long ago graphic designers were the answer to the proverbial questions; 'What's next?' And thanks to our ground-floor co-optation of the personal computer we became gurus of communications and founts of prescience. We knew before anyone else that a dull screen was a bad screen and encouraged engineers and technicians to create software that allowed us to dominate the virtual, visual landscape with bells and whistles. We made the word 'font' a household name. We even allowed Macintosh to tell the world on national TV in the late 1980s that such a species as graphic designers existed, and then had them reveal that the world did not need us anymore. This, of course, was sly subterfuge, because what that classic TV commercial really meant was that only graphic designers can do best with a computer what the average citizen could never hope to achieve.

We entered Internet space before most other visual specialists and before it was possible to stream videos and films, therefore becoming veritable masters (or co-masters) of the dot.com universe. As motion-making programs developed we were the first to introduce typographic animation to the world. We became graphic designer-production-technicians, cornering the market and thus sending the message that we were a force to be reckoned with. We built huge companies in which we were the bosses. We became the producers and authors of content. No longer the eccentrics tucked away in an art department, we were the front men and women – mighty, talented, and well fed.

I, for one, relished being a member of a field that could be counted among the elite. It did wonders for my ego and afforded good cocktail party banter.

'My God, you're a graphic designer,' someone gushed at a wedding. 'I wish that I could become one.' On another occasion a dinner guest breathlessly said

up the whazoo with the most stylish appointments. This helped attract and stimulate the feeding frenzy of entrepreneurial whales that swallowed up independent studios in return for reams of inflated shares. It seemed as though this was the future for some time to come.

But fate is a bastard.

As dot.com turned into not.com and bear turned into bullshit economy, graphic design began to feel the pain. But it is not the first time. During the 1980s a boom real-estate market in the Southwest United States was manna for a newly flourishing graphic design profession. This was the first renaissance of graphic design and also marked as a signpost of increased significance the growth of AIGA chapters throughout the US. Then came downturn and

CLAQUENT

'Graphic design? That must be such a thrilling line of work. Do tell.'

Indeed, as the world learned to detest lawyers and mistrust doctors, graphic designers reached zenith status. The job market couldn't get enough of us. Parents forced their kids to go to design school, and students graduated with high-paying job offers from firms and corporations galore. Of course, many entry-level salaries were obscene by previous standards but comparable with corporate lawyers (and hey, you only live once). Graphic designers were also contributing to the economy in other ways. Certainly in New York we stimulated a stagnant real estate market by renting prime space and renovating

recession. It did not wipe out graphic design, but it was humbled for the next few years. Then the digital revolution hit. The Next Big Thing was a new wave of graphic pioneers, experimenters and theorists doing pioneering, experimental and theoretical design. It was cool to be us. Okay, it is still cool to be us but not as glamorous. The publicity-garnering epoch of typo-centricity known as 'The End of Print' has run its course.

Experimental graphics have become commercial style. And while there is still some buzz about certain developments and people within our field, we're not novelty enough to capture the public's fascination any more. The new media promise to redefine graphic design into

MATS

a multi-tasking-authoring-creative field has proven false. Designers are returning to print and the computer has made many of us into production artists. But the real symptom of decline is simple; it is harder to get work.

In San Francisco, for example, where so much new business depended on dot.coms, there is no work for the hordes of new grads. Elsewhere, there are slowdowns and a sense of foreboding. Of course, this is cyclical. And there is no reason to believe that graphic design will suffer in the long run. We all know that everyone's got to have design. But what it does mean is that the Next Big Thing is not pushing pixels, making posters, designing books, or even constructing websites. The Next Big Thing is....

Steven Heller,
'The Next Small Thing',
from *Eye*, no. 42, vol. 11,
winter 2001

Stephan Bundi began his career as an apprentice at Young & Rubicam, before setting up his own studio in 1975 in Berne, Switzerland, where he also teaches at the Hochschule für Gestaltung (Design Academy). A dedicated and demanding graphic artist, he speaks here of the commitment to graphics that is needed to produce truly innovative projects.

The Power of the Hand in the Age of the Computer

It seems that any discussion of graphic design must touch on the subject of computer technology, the impact it has had on design and reproduction techniques, and the way it has changed visual communication. This technology has also had a social impact: designers, for

the most part, can no longer work in isolation from the technological developments occurring around them. Rather, designers, like members of just about every other profession, have come to rely on computers, peripheral devices and software. Although this relationship with new and ever-changing technology significantly boosts designers' productivity, it also puts them at the mercy of the hardware and software manufacturers and developers, and makes full networking with customers and suppliers an absolute necessity. Universal availability is having a major impact on the designer's rhythm of work and creative output. Computers have given graphic designers new possibilities for creating playful, sophisticated typography. Unfortunately legibility often suffers as a result. Electronic manipulation techniques have spawned new, unfamiliar visual worlds. We now sometimes see highly specialized advertising agencies and studios combining textual and visual messages to create posters which both provide information and can be enjoyed as works of art. On the whole, the visual language used in these posters relies heavily on graphic, typographic and photographic elements. Figurative elements in the form of drawn or painted illustrations are seldom, if ever, used. Despite the awesome power of this new technology, some designers still choose to do without it. They reserve their computer for office work or, at most, for the pre-printing stage. These few stalwarts prefer to hone their drawing and painting skills, the basic

DANGER

tools of their trade, combining them with a flair for visual communication. The result is surprising, striking images.

The work of these designers is to be found in *Graphis Posters*, a publication which for a quarter of a century has surveyed the whole world of poster design. Its pages have featured the works of the masters, graphic designers such as Paul Brühwiler, Seymour Chwast, Heinz Edelmann, Anke Feuchtenberger, Milton Glaser, Hans Hillmann, Claude Kuhn, Istvan Orosz, Lanny Sommese, Waldemar Swierzy, Franticek Starowieyski, Niklaus Troxler, Tomi Ungerer and Henning Wagenbreth. Typically, their creations appear in the most recent as well as the earliest editions. Demand for their work seems to have remained undiminished over the decades. Pixel technology offers no substitute for their unique signature and the way they interpret and represent the issues.

In the fine arts, drawing and painting appear to have been superseded or are only accepted as fringe activities. In contrast, for those of us in visual communications they still constitute a valid – and vibrant – form. Figurative representation, regardless of how abstract, is virtually a must when it comes to communicating clearly. Anyone who believes that figurative drawing is outmoded should ask whether designers will really have sufficient scope for putting across the message if they do without figurative representation altogether. Won't physiognomy in its broadest sense

6O

continue to fascinate? Can the current trend of ignoring the actual subject in favor of vague ciphers overlaid with difficult-to-read typographic elements outlast the fatigue that continual bouts with irony inspire?

A drawing is a creative work and interpretation rolled into one. It is not reproduction in a narrow sense, but

48 always involves the representation of an idea, the tangible communication of a vision, using optical abstraction to bring content to life. A designer's work is driven and guided by an interplay of constants and variables; the object to be communicated and the knowledge of how it can be represented are the constants; the designer's personal touch and the element of chance and subjective interpretation are the variables. The more freely a designer works, the more clearly this process is reflected in the results. Honest communications designers always interpret the theme rather than themselves.

Despite the many different possibilities on offer, visual languages created by electronic means are often rather superficial and homogeneous. By contrast, hand-drawn representations, 'imperfect' as they are, have a certain quality and charm which demand

3IFUR

attention. The form and content of a hand-drawn or painted design can be so provocative that the poster remains imprinted on the viewer's memory simply because it stands out clearly on a billboard full of standard fare.

If the viewer's curiosity is sufficiently aroused for them to go to the event or buy the product advertised, then the poster has done its job.

In a Schiller play for which I recently designed a poster, William Tell says that a strong man is strongest when he works alone. Designers who buck the trend by producing hand-drawn or painted work have to be strong, because their decisions cannot be easily rationalized. They cannot constantly call up their work on screen and reorganize it, so delegating to other people is seldom possible. To a certain extent they have to be totally and personally involved in a project, from the first sketches to the reproduction stage. Working alone can make a designer feel isolated and insecure – but can also bring euphoria and great contentment.

Stephan Bundi,
in *Graphis Poster Annual*, 2000

3IFUR

FURTHER READING

General Works

50 Years, Swiss Posters Selected by the Federal Department of Home Affairs, 1941–1990, Geneva, 1991

Ades, Dawn, and Benton, Tim, Art and Power: Europe under the Dictators, 1930–1945, London, 1996

Ades, Dawn, The 20th-Century Poster: Design of the Avant Garde, New York, 1984

Aynsley, Jeremy, Graphic Design in Germany 1890–1945, London, 2000

Bellantoni, Jeff and Woolman, Matt, Type in Motion: Innovations in Digital Graphics, London, 2000

Branczyk, Alexander (ed.), Emotional Digital: A Sourcebook of Contemporary Typographics, London, 2001

Frantz Kery, Patricia, Art Deco Graphics, London, 2002

Harper, Laurel, Radical Graphics, Graphic Radicals, San Francisco, 1999

Heller, Steven and Ballance, Georgette (eds), Graphic Design History, New York, 2001

Heller, Steven and Chwast, Seymour, Graphic Style: from Victorian to Post-Modern, London, 1988

Heller, Steven and Ilic, Mirko, Icons of Graphic Design, London, 2001

Hollis, Richard, Graphic Design: A Concise History, London, rev. ed. 2002

Friedl, Friedrich, Ott, Nicolaus, and Stein, Bernard, Typography: An Encyclopedic Survey of Type Design and Techniques throughout History, New York, 1998

Küsters, Christian, and King, Emily, Restart: New Systems in Graphic Design, London, 2001

Livingston, Alan and Isabella, The Thames & Hudson Dictionary of Graphic Design and Designers, London, new ed. 2003

Meggs, Philip B., History of Graphic Design, New York, 3rd ed. 1998

Pack, Susan, Film Posters of the Russian Avant-Garde, Cologne and New York, 1985

Purvis, Alston W., Dutch Graphic Design, 1918–1945, New York, 1992

Remington, Roger and Hodik, Barbara J., Nine Pioneers in American Graphic Design, Cambridge, Mass., 1989

Rothschild, Deborah, Lupton, Ellen, and Goldstein, Darra, Graphic Design in the Mechanical Age: Selections from the Merrill C. Berman Collection, New Haven, 1998

Triggs, Teal, The Typographic Experiment: Radical Innovation in Contemporary Type Design, London, 2003

Weill, Alain, The Poster: A Worldwide Survey and History, Boston, 1985

Monographs

Blackwell, Lewis, The End of Print: the Graphic Design of David Carson, London and San Francisco, 1995

Farrelly, Liz, April Greiman: Floating Ideas into Time and Space, London, 1998

Farrelly, Liz, Tibor Kalman: Design and Undesign, London, 1998

Grundberg, Andy, Brodovitch, New York, 1989

Levenson, Bob, Bill Bernbach's Book: A History of Advertising that Changed the History of Advertising, New York, 1987

Lissitzky-Küppers, Sophie, El Lissitzky, London, 1992

Maeda, John, Maeda@Media, London, 2000

Massin, Robert, Letter and Image, trans. Caroline Hillier and Vivienne Menkes, London and New York, 1970

Mouron, Henri, A.M. Cassandre, trans. Michael Taylor, New York, 1985

Passuth, Krisztina, Moholy-Nagy, London, 1987

Rand, Paul, Paul Rand: A Designer's Art, New Haven and London, 1985

Sarfis, Thierry and Maruszewska, Ewa (eds), Henryk Tomaszewski, Graphismes et pédagogie, Paris, 1995

Wozencroft, Jon, The Graphic Language of Neville Brody, London, 1988

LIST OF ILLUSTRATIONS

The following abbreviations have been used: **a** above, **b** below, **c** centre, **l** left, **r** right.

COVER

Front (detail) *F. Virtual, Fuse 5*, FontShop International 1992, by Neville Brody. Taken from *The Graphic Language of Neville Brody 2*, by Jon Wozencroft, London, 1994.

Spine Monograms of the artists of the Vienna Secession.

Back Gustav Klutsis, 'The USSR is leading the workers of the world', 1931, poster.

OPENING

1 A. M. Cassandre, cover of price list for the wine merchants Nicolas, 1936.

2 'Nectar Sitting Down', poster for Nicolas wines, after Dransy, *c.* 1925.

3 Orsi, 'Nectar', poster for Nicolas wines, 1929. Risacher Publishers.

4 Cover of price list for Nicolas wines, 1930.

5 Georges Lepape, poster design for Nicolas, 1953, gouache on cardboard. Private collection.

6–7 A. M. Cassandre, poster for Nicolas, 1935.

9 Milton Glaser, design for Babycurls typeface, *c.* 1970.

CHAPTER 1

10 Henry van de Velde, poster for the dried food company Tropon, 1898.

11l Manoli cigarette box, early 20th century (designer unknown).

11r Lucian Bernhard, Manoli cigarette boxes, 1911–14.

12 Ottmar Mergenthaler (seated) demonstrating the Blower Linotype to Whitelaw Reid, 3 July 1886, engraving. Courtesy of the Mergenthaler Linotype Company, Melville, NY.

13 Poster printing workshop, late 19th century.

14a William Morris, title page for *The Tale of King Constans Emperor of Byzance*, Kelmscott Press, 1894 or 1896.

14b William Morris, photograph.

15a Otto Eckmann, decorative motif based on John Ruskin's name.

15b Arthur Mackmurdo, title page for *Wren's City Churches*, 1883.

16a Aubrey Beardsley, 'Keynotes Series', 1896, poster.

16b Aubrey Beardsley, 'Avenue Theatre', 1894, poster.

17a Beggarstaff Brothers, 'A Trip to China Town', 1895, poster.

17b Herbert McNair, Margaret and Frances Macdonald, 'The Glasgow Institute of the Fine Arts', 1896, poster.

18l Jules Chéret, 'Saxoléine lamp oil', 1891, poster.

18r Stage curtain at Les Ambassadeurs music hall, Paris, photograph, *c.* 1895.

19a Henri de Toulouse-Lautrec, 'Moulin Rouge', 1891, poster.

19b Photograph of Henri de Toulouse-Lautrec and Charles Zidler in front of (inset) Jules Chéret's poster 'Bal au Moulin Rouge', colour poster, 1889.

20a Comparison of the typefaces Grasset (upper row) and Auriol (lower row).

20c Double-page spread from *Histoire des Quatre Fils Aymon*, illustrated by Eugène Grasset. Private collection.

21r Alphonse Mucha, 'Gismonda-Bernhardt', 1895, theatre poster.

21bl Eugène Grasset, poster artwork for the Salon des Cent, 1894.

22al Théophile Alexandre Steinlen, 'Vigeanne pure sterilized milk', 1894, poster.

22ac Leonetto Cappiello, 'Chocolat Klaus', 1903, poster.

22ar Pierre Bonnard, 'France-Champagne', 1891, poster.

22bl O'Galop (Marius Roussillon), 'Le coup de la semelle Michelin', *c.* 1910, poster.

22br Adolfo Hohenstein, 'Phosphorus-free matches', *c.* 1900, poster.

24a Emile Berchmans, 'Le Bock de Koekelberg', poster artwork, 1896.

24b Henry van de Velde, 'Tropon, the most concentrated foodstuff', 1898, poster.

25a Privat-Livemont, 'Bec Auer', 1896, poster for gas company.

RAPPELLE-TOI

ÆŒÇCᴱCƎ

ÆŒÇCᴱCƎ

ÆŒÇCᴱCƎ

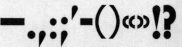

QU'IL FAUT

SUIVRE
LA
MODE
TYPOGRAPHIQUE

ABCDEFGHIJ

QRSTUVWXY

DEBERNY ET PEIGNOT

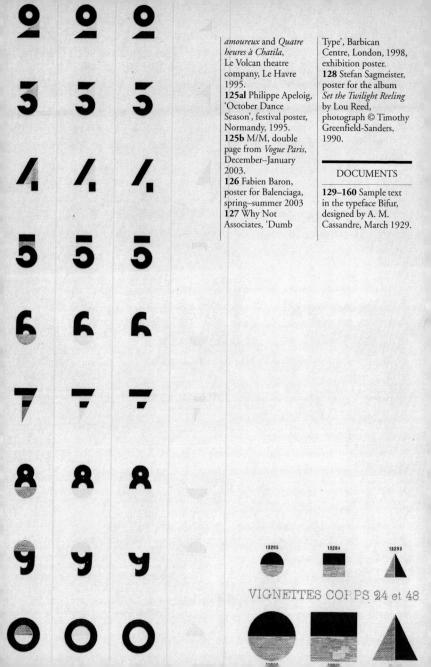

DOCUMENTS

VIGNETTES CORPS 24 et 48

INDEX

LE BIFUR

CASSANDRE

PICTURE CREDITS

All illustrations belong to private collections (photos Patrick Léger/Gallimard) with the following exceptions: Bridgeman Art Library: 14c. Heinz Company Archives, Pittsburgh, PA: 37b. John Maeda: 114r. Willy Maywald: 63. Swann Galleries, New York: 18l, 19a, 21r, 21bl, 22al, 22ac, 34l, 35, 44, 45l, 59, 67, 72a, 72b, 73, 78, 81r, 82r, 83, 90a, 91r, 93, 95, 97a, 106a, 106b, 111r, 114l. Viollet Collection: 19b.

ACKNOWLEDGMENTS

The author and publishers wish to thank Nicholas D. Lowry, Percy Lehning, Guillaume Sebag, Florence Robert, and especially Richard Avedon, Anthon Beeke, Pierre Bernard, Robert Delpire, Laurent Fétis, Milton Glaser, April Greiman, Steven Heller, Holger Matthies, M/M, Gunter Rambow, Stefan Sagmeister, Makoto Saito, Paula Scher, Ruben Steeman, Studio Dumbar, Niklaus Troxler, Michael Worthington, Tadanori Yokoo.

Lucy Chalmers.

Alain Weill is a former director of the Musée de la Publicité in Paris
and an expert in graphic design and advertising. His many books include
The Poster: A Worldwide Survey and History (Boston, 1985) and
Chocolate Posters (New York, 2002). He is also a restaurant critic.

To Jo Vargas

ACHEVÉ

D'IMPRIMER

le 30 Mars 1929

sur les presses

des

FONDERIES

DEBERNY

PEIGNOT

18, Rue Ferrus

PARIS XIV⁰

Translated from the French by Barbara Mellor

First published in the United Kingdom in 2004 by
Thames & Hudson Ltd, 181A High Holborn, London WC1V 7QX

British Library Cataloguing-in-Publication Data
A catalogue record for this book is available from the British Library
ISBN 0–500–30116–6
Printed and bound in Italy by Editoriale Lloyd, Trieste